25 Short Stories

for

Cruise Ship Travelers

First published in Great Britain in 2020 by Midealuck Publishing Ltd.

The right of Christian Stahl to be identified as the Author of the work has been asserted by him in accordance with the Copyright.

All rights reserved.

License Notice

In no way is it legal to reproduce, duplicate, download, or transmit any part of this document in either electronic means or in printed format without the consent of the author or publisher. Recording of this publication is strictly prohibited and any storage of this document is not allowed unless with written permission from the publisher.

All Rights Reserved

The information provided herein is stated to be truthful and consistent, in that any liability, in terms of inattention or otherwise, by any usage or abuse of any policies, processes, or directions contained within is the solitary and utter responsibility of the recipient reader. Under no circumstances will any legal responsibility or blame be held against the publisher or author for any reparation, damages, or monetary loss due to the information herein, either directly or indirectly. The information herein is offered for informational purposes solely and is universal as so. Any name and content in this book is fiction and not related to any real events or persons.

Table of Contents

Marooned
A Cruise on the Nile
The Breach
A Cruel Odyssey
The Casino
The Space Cruise
The Ghost Cruise Liner
High Waves
The Cherry Blossom Stones
A Special Cooking Course
Bermuda Marriage
Encounter in the South China Sea
Nagano Gold
Dining with the Captain
The Stowaway
Strangers on an Ocean Liner
She Jumped on Her Own
Escape from Venice
The Greatest Show on Earth
The Haunting
Forever on Board
Finding Lasting Love
The Vegan Passenger
The Tourist Guide
Table Sharing
The Captain's Compartment

Marooned

Katie pushed her toes into the fine yellow sand, her eyes on the meagre fire that crackled and popped, a glowing greenly with too much salt and doing absolutely nothing to keep her warm. Her hair hung down her back, long and honey-yellow, bleached to a crisp by the incessant sunlight. She had lost her hair tie during the storm that had washed her up on the island.

Her mouth was dry, dehydration settling in a long time ago, her skin tight and crusted with salt, her lips sticking together and cracked to the point of bleeding no matter how many times she licked them.

Movement caught her eye, and she looked up as Richard approached. His hair had grown longer during their time here, falling around his cheeks and stringy brown like mouse tails that covered his dark eyes unless he pushed it out of the way. He had gotten skinny during their time here, losing all the excess weight and muscle from walking around searching for water and hunting for food for them – all with little success.

He gave her a thin smile when she looked down, seeing that he was empty-handed.

"Nothing?" she asked, unable to keep the disappointment from her voice.

He shook his head and sat beside her. "Maybe Elias will have more luck," he offered. His throat had the same grittiness of the sand. Katie pressed her lips together, looking up. The island was small; it took a day to walk around the entire border by her best guess. There were trees growing, and a small rise in the center. There had to be water *somewhere*, she reasoned. Even if it was deep underground, it was somewhere. The island was subtropical, and humidity clung to them like rainwater even though there wasn't anything fresh to drink. Palm trees with sparse amounts of coconuts had been the only source of water for quite some time.

She wrapped her arms more tightly around her knees and set her chin on top of them, sighing. They shouldn't be here, should never have gotten onto that stupid yacht.

They'd met at a bar in the San Diego marina – Katie and Richard and Ivan, a high-roller who dressed flashy and smiled like a salesman, with slick black hair and eyes the color of blue stained glass. Richard was good at making friends with rich people, and still young and lucky enough to get away with seeking a good time over a safe one.

So when, after an evening making friends and a day as tour guide, Ivan had said he wanted to sail across the Pacific, that he had a crew and a boat at the ready, and invited Richard and Katie along – well, it seemed like a perfect opportunity for adventure.

Looking back on it now, Katie knew she should have been more suspicious from the get-go. The yacht itself had been gigantic, closer to a cruise ship than anything she had expected. It had glimmered white as a jewel in the sunlight atop the crystal blue water, with two separate pools on the top deck, and a banquet hall, and even a ballroom and miniature casino on one of the floors. She remembered the tour of the boat, in awe of the hanging chandeliers in the ballroom that swayed on the gentle tide, the deep red carpets in the hallways and the low ambient lighting. The yacht had several floors, all of them dripping with luxury. The bed in their room was huge and the walls were a deep burnished golden color, the carpet red, and made her think that she had stepped into a Vegas hotel suite.

"Are we expecting anyone else?" she asked, when there was champagne in her hand and a squirrelly little man crooning a romantic ballad from the piano placed at the bar next to the pool.

Ivan grinned and shook his head. That should have been the second sign, she thought bitterly.

Despite the size of the yacht, Katie couldn't recall seeing more than a dozen separate faces the entire time they'd been sailing. Ivan spent most of his time in conversation with the captain, a dark-skinned man with a shock of white hair and a thick mustache that moved when he spoke, and when he wasn't there, he was often on deck with a drink in his hand and a phone to his ear. Katie wasn't sure what to make of it – he had invited them along, after all, surely he wouldn't have done that if he didn't want to spend time with them.

Questions to the crew went avoided or unanswered. Most of them barely spoke any English, and Katie didn't know enough Russian to question them properly.

She had overheard the fight one night, when Richard was passed out from too many drinks and snoring on their – admittedly, very comfortable – bed in their room. She wandered the dark halls, barefoot, her hair tied up in a loose bun so that she could get some of the cool ocean breeze on her neck. She'd paused, outside the outer door to the banquet hall when she heard a short, sharp noise of alarm. Not a scream of danger, but an angry sound.

She leaned in and peered through the window. Ivan was there, pacing, his thin face red with outrage as he gestured wildly between the captain, and a priest, and a third man who looked more military than a worker on the ship. He was yelling, in Russian, she didn't understand what he was saying, but she was sure it couldn't be good. It wasn't good.

When they'd arrived in Tahiti – several days late, according to the priest, who was the only one Katie had found who could speak enough English for a decent conversation besides Ivan– they'd been ordered to stay offshore and drop anchor outside the port. The authorities were called, and there had been another heated discussion.

"This is outrageous!" Ivan's angry words still rang in her head, when it got particularly quiet. "I only need supplies for my ship and my crew, and then I can be on my way."

"We understand that Sir, but you don't have any money."

And Katie knew she was staring, but she couldn't help herself. Richard was more laid back than she was and didn't observe the world with as critical an eye. Ivan's cagey attitude, the sullen skeleton crew, and the antsy behavior of the authorities all stacked together in her head like puzzle pieces.

"Are there any other places to stock up, if we can't resupply here?" she had asked.

The priest – a man who had introduced himself as Father Elias – had smiled at her and patted her hand. "I'm sure there is," he assured her. "Ivan is a resourceful man. Don't fret."

She should have fretted.

"You are welcome to dock with us," the Tahitian man had said, "but you will be held while we contact your country of origin, as well as your port of call, to make sure everything clears correctly."

Katie had wanted to leave, then. They had their passports and were essentially tourists – they could have figured out a way to get home. Clearly associating with Ivan wasn't going to do them any favors, if the building bad feeling in Katie's gut was anything to go by. Richard didn't want to leave, though – he had been seduced by the top shelf liquor and the giant bed and Ivan's charming smile.

She should have been more adamant. Or just left by herself. She was smart, she could have figured something out. But no, of course, she couldn't leave Richard. And then they left Tahiti and started heading in a different direction than West, and no one could or would tell her where they were going, not even Father Elias, Katie had seen the writing on the wall. Ivan was in a black mood, scowling at everything, snipping at her whenever they were in the same room.

Which brought them back to the island. Ivan had caught her stashing food away, certain that at some point the supplies would run out. She'd wanted to keep enough for her and Richard to survive. They were the outsiders, after all, and the ones that would be taken care of last, after the crew. Objectively, Katie didn't even blame Ivan for that.

He'd come into their bedroom in the middle of the night, with the captain and that nameless military man. Katie and Richard were put on a tiny life boat in the middle of a storm and pushed off the edge of the yacht, forced to battle choppy waves and freezing rain. She had been certain that they were going to die.

They hadn't died. By the grace of God or whatever held sway in the universe, they were here, barely clinging to life. They had no food, no water, no additional clothes. Katie had been wearing her pajamas at the time, no shoes or socks, and the island got cold at night. Richard was worse off, in just a t-shirt and his underwear which was clumped with sand and so dirty she knew it had to be uncomfortable.

They had been stuck on the island for a couple of days when the first body washed up. It was the piano player, still in his nice suit, cold and pale and dead. Then, a few minutes later, the captain. The crew. The military man, and Ivan himself. All of them, drowned from what she could tell, scattered amongst the driftwood, the broken pieces of the yacht's white hull.

There had been some food, at least, to keep them from starving.

Elias had been the only survivor. It had taken almost three minutes of mouth to mouth to get him to cough water from his lungs, and he was weak and dizzy, but he had survived, and told them that the same storm that had swept them to this island had gotten worse, and capsized the ship.

There were birds on the island, and small rodents, but they were too quick, and Katie and Richard didn't have the skills for traps or the ability to hunt them. The food that had washed up was soaked through and everything tasted like fish and salt. The only liquids were half-drunk bottles of alcohol and one single plastic jug of water, which they drank from as sparingly as they could, supplementing the water with what they could split from the few coconuts that grew upon the island.

They were running out of options.

Richard stood, drawing her attention, and went out towards the shore. Katie rose, and followed him, as he took a large stone in his hand and set it on the beach, amidst the halves of the coconuts they had split open and drained.

It took her only a moment to realize what he was doing. She smiled to herself, but it was a small thing, her lips too dry to really give it her all. She helped him set up the first giant 'S' on the beach, and then began with the 'O'. Between all the debris from the ship, and the rocks on the shore, they had enough material to make a large enough 'S.O.S.' that she hoped it was visible from far away, or perhaps above. Wherever they were, no one else had come by this way, but maybe someone would see them from the air and call for help.

The fire died while they were working, and Elias returned as Katie sat down by the smoking twigs and watched Richard try to relight it, shivering in the cold breeze. He was empty-handed too – the jug he had taken with him was as dry as when he'd left, and his defeated expression told her all she needed to know.

"We've got a few more days of water left, tops," Richard said, mouth twisted in concentration as he tried to get the fire to light again. It was difficult, despite how dry the wood was. The breeze pulled at Katie's dry skin and dirty clothes and made her shiver, curling up more tightly on herself.

Elias nodded. His face was coated with sweat from his trip, and he pulled at his thick priest garments, parting his cassock to reveal black slacks beneath, fanning the fabric to cool himself down. Katie watched him slip off his shoes and socks and sink his feet into the cold sand.

"We can't stay here," he said, looking out towards the remaining debris of the ship. He bit his lower lip, brow furrowed in thought. "Perhaps we can try to build a raft."

Katie laughed, short and bitter. "I don't know the first thing about building a raft."

"We have to try," Elias said. "There's no help coming, not where we are."

Katie eyed him. She was used to seeing him smiling; he had a round face, and no hair on his head, and the genteel manner of an old man who had seen so much that it had only made him kind. His stricken expression, the dark circles under his eyes, and the pallor on his skin made him look sick.

She sighed and nodded. "In the morning, then." They piled together for sleep, sharing body heat since it was so cold, and Richard hadn't managed to light the fire again. Dawn came swiftly, lighting the sky in pretty oranges and pinks. It was beautiful here, she had to admit, and she might have even enjoyed it had the three of them been in a position to think of anything but survival.

She gathered vines from the sparse foliage growing on the island while Elias and Richard worked together to find scraps of debris that were large enough to bind together and make a raft. It was small, and uncomplicated. Richard was able to find a large plastic tarp to wrap around the wood and metal to stop it soaking through with water, making a pallet that was just large enough for all three to sit on.

They brought the water container with them, and what was left of their food, and set sail. Their combined weight made it so that the raft sat about an inch below the surface, but it floated, and that was all they could hope for. Richard and Katie had been given oars for their lifeboat. The boat itself was shredded, pieces of it added for buoyancy and to keep everything airtight.

It felt like they were floating on a cloud, and a wing and a prayer. The sun blazed down on them, burning hot, and while the water kept their feet cold and wrinkling, Katie could practically feel her skin burning and see Richard and Elias turning red.

They finished their food on the second day. They had no way of knowing what direction would lead them to land quickest, since none of them had any idea where they were. Seagulls cried above them, but sometimes when the light hit just right, they looked like vultures.

They were going to pick their bones clean. She thought of this with a cool detachment. Maybe no one would ever find them. It would only take one solid wave to take them under and wash them down to the bottom of the sea. They didn't have the strength to fight the current. If they sank, then that was the end of it.

She eyed the growing storm clouds on the horizon with dreadful certainty.

Richard rowed for most of the way, Elias taking over when he physically couldn't keep it up anymore. Katie steered with her own oar, pointing them West and squinting into the sunset. Her fingers cramped around the handle of the oar, her shoulders tense and burned to a crisp. Her hair was so brittle it fell out in clumps, and she wished she could shave the whole damn thing off.

They ran out of water on the third day.

She expected it, but still, the last few droplets that would slake their thirst disappeared with a finality that made her think of her inevitable watery grave. Richard had taken it, since he was the one spending the most energy keeping them going. There was no notion of saliva, or even, she considered briefly, drinking their own urine.

"We're going to die," she said quietly.

Richard glared at her. "No, we're not," he said adamantly. "Don't think like that."

"We don't have enough water, Richard. We don't have any food."

Richard merely shook his head. He had always been more optimistic, willing to believe that everything would work out eventually. How he could still think that way, she would never know. She supposed it wasn't going to be much of an issue, either way.

On the fourth day, Katie and Richard woke to find that they were alone. Her eyes widened in panic, and she looked around the raft, in case Elias had rolled off during the night and was trying to catch up with them. She couldn't see him at all.

"Richard!" she cried. "Where is he?"
Richard's face was pale beneath the sunburn, and he met her eyes.

"I feel asleep," he added guiltily. "I didn't see...."
He looked to the side, and his eyes widened. "Look."

In the spot where Elias had been, was a single bottle of water wrapped up in Elias' cassock. There was no note, but it seemed obvious what he had done. Katie had no water in her to cry, but her shoulders trembled and she pressed a hand to her mouth, as Richard took the bottle with shaking hands and drank. He offered her some of the warm liquid. It was drinkable, the bottle had been sealed.

"How long do you think he was holding onto this?" Richard asked, as she handed it back. She had forced herself to only take a mouthful.

"I don't know," she replied. "I guess as long as he thought we might need it."

Katie closed her eyes, sending a silent 'Thank you' to the man that she had only known for so short a time, that had sacrificed himself to give them one last fighting chance, one last shred of hope. She hoped that he had passed away peacefully, that he felt no pain.

She was still thinking of Elias when her eyes lifted, and she saw a plume of smoke on the horizon. Her eyes widened, and she grabbed Richard's shoulder, nodding towards it. "Look!" she rasped. She wasn't sure what the origin was – a ship, or another island, but it was a sign of life. Richard nodded and Katie steered their raft towards it, and took Elias' cassock, waving it above her head.

The blaring sound of a ship's horn made her cry in relief. They had been seen. The ship slowed, and angled towards them, and a moment later Katie saw the bright blob of a yellow lifeboat heading their way.

"Thank God," Richard breathed, collapsing to his knees.

No, she thought. Thank Elias. Because of his sacrifice, by rolling into the water and letting himself drown and leaving behind that single scrap of additional water, they had managed to find somewhere safe. Because of him, they were alive, and were being rescued.

There were three men on the lifeboat, and they gathered Katie and Richard up, and gave them water and small granola bars to sate their hunger. "You look like you've had quite the adventure," the leader said.

He was an older man, with a thick beard and dark eyes.

Katie laughed bitterly, and said, "You don't know the half of it."

A Cruise on the Nile

'Well go on, show me.'

Jerry lifted his shirt. Barbara could see the rumpled, crescent-shaped scar running from below his navel up to just below his ribs.

'It makes me feel weird,' Jerry said. 'Like I'm walking around with a secret. Someone else's kidney is in there.'

'It's your kidney now,' said Barbara. 'Come on, I've got a surprise for you.'

Jerry followed Barbara into the study. He was a heavy-set man, approaching sixty, his grey hair starting to thin. But his green eyes were bright and alert – his best feature, Barbara always said. Barbara had aged better. She was slim and fit and moved quickly. She'd cut her honey-brown hair short for the first time two weeks ago and still occasionally lifted a hand to touch it self-consciously. Outside, the afternoon sun was beating against the house. Jerry, who'd lived his whole life in Minnesota, hated the heat. But what Barbara wanted, Barbara got. So two years ago they'd moved back to her hometown of Naples, Florida. Then Jerry got sick.

'Look,' said Barbara, and she handed Jerry a folded piece of paper.

'What's this?'

'You remember I was saying we deserved a holiday? You know, leave the country, be somewhere totally different. To put all this behind us.'

'Yeah?'

'Open it.'

It was a brochure for a cruise along the Nile. On the inside page was a picture of the ship, and written above it: "Travel through time in style and comfort".

'This looks like a pretty old brochure,' said Jerry, peering at the photographs.

'Oh no, they just dress the boat up like it's the 1920s. The crew as well. You know, British colonial style. It seemed like fun.'

Barbara stood with her back to the desk, which was swamped by a disorderly stack of correspondence – doctor's appointments, scans, letters from their insurance company.

'Yeah,' said Jerry, trying to smile. 'Looks like fun. Thank you, sweetheart. You always know just what to do.'

Egypt, Jerry thought to himself. *Perfect. More sun and heat.*

When they arrived, Jerry's first thought was that their tour guide was taking the 1920s theme too far. He bowed and scraped as though a bad word from Jerry or Barbara would get him whipped. He was a small, lean man, his uniform perfectly pressed.

'Welcome,' he said. 'My name is Ammon, please let me help you.'

Jerry handed over the suitcases and they followed Ammon up the ramp.

The ship certainly looked like something out of the 1920s. It was a long barge with two broad decks, and it sat low in the gleaming waters of the Nile. The decks were enclosed by elaborate wrought iron railings, painted white, with soft curtains that could be drawn in the heat of the day. Some of the guests could already be seen sitting at private tables, attended to by the crew. On the far shore, tall palm trees stirred in the breeze. People hurried along the riverfront promenade, coming and going from the bustling modern city of Luxor.

'May I say,' said Ammon as he led them towards their cabin. 'You have chosen the perfect itinerary. Luxor to Aswan is the perfect way to experience the Nile. For myself, I cannot believe my good fortune to have this job. To be paid a salary to experience such wonders every day.'

Barbara smiled, pleased with her choice. The sight of the crew, in their neat uniforms and stylish caps, thrilled her. They passed by the lounge, and Barbara paused to look inside. The room was exquisite; clad in dark wood panels and lined with beautiful old leather couches. The sunlight filtered through wooden shutters so that the whole room was suffused with a soft glow. *Like stepping into a photograph*, she thought.

'Barbara?' said Jerry.

There were shouts from the crew and the boat rocked slightly, and Barbara reached out to steady herself. Ammon smiled back at her. His teeth were very white.

'We have cast off,' he said. 'Today we sail only a very short distance, to Karnak. You will want plenty of time to explore the ancient temple.'

'What about the historic hotel?' Barbara asked, reaching into her pocket for her brochure. 'Karnak's where we stay in the historic hotel, isn't it?'

'Here is your cabin,' said Ammon.

Ammon pushed back the wooden shutters and the sun flooded in. He stood expectantly at the door.

'Oh,' said Jerry, reaching into his pocket. 'I've only got American dollars.'

Ammon took the five-dollar bill, smiling. 'I'll leave you to rest.'

'Didn't he say he was on a salary?' Jerry grumbled, once Ammon had gone. 'What's he doing taking a tip?'

'That's probably just the way they do things here.'

'Can you see if they've got air con in this cabin?' said Jerry, wiping his forehead.

Jerry lowered his camera.

'Stand to the left,' he said.

Barbara took a step to the right.

'No, *your* left.'

Barbara stood still, smiling, framed by the hieroglyph-inscribed pillars of the Hypostyle Hall at Karnak.

'Did you get it?' Barbara called. Her voice echoed off the towering pillars.

The shadows of the great columns fell across the pale, ancient pavers. Jerry clicked back through the photographs he had taken earlier that day: Barbara standing under the rough cliffs of the Valley of the Kings and Queens, and on the shore of the Nile, the sunrise spilling across the water. Jerry felt faint. Maybe it was the sun, or maybe just being in these ancient places. The way time seemed to stretch here in Egypt made him dizzy.

Jerry?' said Barbara. 'He's had an operation,' she added, explaining, to Ammon.

'We could go back to the boat,' said Ammon. 'There will be a fantastic Galabeya party on board tonight.'

Jerry shook his head. 'I'm ready for the hotel.'

They made the crossing to the far shore in a felucca; a nimble little boat with a single, blade-like sail. The ochre-colored hills towered above the city. They made Jerry feel uneasy, as if at any moment they might slip and cover the city in ancient rubble. When they landed, Barbara started up the stone steps towards the hotel, but Ammon hurried past and blocked her way.

'Please, Mrs. Shilling, this way.

'But that's the hotel,' said Barbara. 'Its picture is in the brochure.'

Ammon smiled. 'The hotel is closed for renovation.'

'It doesn't look closed,' said Jerry.

'Please, come this way. We have another hotel, just as good.'

Ammon waved a taxi over. Before Barbara could protest, her bag was lifted from her hands and into the taxi. Jerry let himself be guided into the car. He tried to keep in mind what Barbara had said that morning. *That's probably just the way they do things here.*

The new hotel didn't look much like a hotel, more like a large house.

'Where's the hotel sign?' said Jerry.

'Ah, this is a private hotel,' said Ammon.

'I don't see any other tourists, Barbara,' Jerry whispered.

It was true. There were lots of people milling about, but they all seemed to be locals.

'I guess we're getting an authentic experience,' said Barbara.

Their room was even smaller than their cabin. The moment they stepped inside, the door swung shut.

'Ammon?' said Jerry. He hurried to the door, but their guide was gone. The corridor was empty, only their bags were stacked outside their door. 'Is anyone there?'

'Jerry, I have a bad feeling about this,' said Barbara. Jerry leaned against the doorframe, breathing heavily. 'Jerry?'

He slipped into her arms. 'I think I got too much sun,' he said.

Barbara pulled him to the bed. He was so heavy she thought for a moment he wouldn't make it, but then he fell across her knees. He was asleep within moments. Barbara sat in the dark little room, her heart pounding in her chest, trying to ignore the faint sounds of animals scuffling in the rafters above her. She tried to move, but Jerry was too heavy. She was pinned in place. A noise came, just outside their door. Barbara looked up and noticed for the first time there was no look on the door.

'Hello?' she forced herself to say, trying to keep the fear from her voice. 'Is someone there?'

She could hear someone breathing. But no one answered. *I have to try to stay awake*, she thought.

The sound of knocking on the door woke them both. Barbara gave a little shout of fright as the door opened. Morning sunlight flooded in, and Ammon stood in the doorway, smiling.

'I hope you had a restful night, Mr. and Mrs. Shilling.'

The rest of their trip, Barbara would tell their friends later, was perfect. Barbara and Jerry took things at their own pace, not rushing like they had on that first day.

'Until we arrived in Aswan,' Barbara would explain. 'And then Ammon… well, it was uncomfortable. I feel sorry for him now. He'd been walking around with this secret.'

Arriving in Aswan, as they walked down the ramp Barbara cast a wistful glance back at the boat.

'I feel like everything back home is going to feel so normal by comparison,' she said.

'Looks like someone wants to say goodbye,' said Jerry.

Ammon was hurrying after them. His uniform, usually perfectly pressed, looked ruffled.

'I am sad to be saying goodbye to two such generous guests,' he said.

Jerry sighed and reached into his pocket for a five-dollar bill.

'Please,' said Ammon. 'I am sorry, Mr. Shilling, but can you spare a little more? My family and I are in a bad situation.' Ammon glanced nervously back at the boat. 'Please, sir.'

'Go on, Jerry,' said Barbara. 'Ammon's been so good to us.'

Jerry fished in his pockets again. 'That's everything I have on me.'

Ammon quickly hid the money in his coat pocket before walking back onto the boat.

Two weeks after Jerry and Barbara returned home, the phone calls started. They came late at night, from another time zone. Then letters and postcards started arriving from towns all along the Nile, written in halting English.

'There was nothing threatening,' Barbara would say to her friends. 'It was like they wanted just to connect with us. To be friends. But we had no idea how to write back.'

At this point, Jerry would always lean across the table. 'Then I looked at my credit card statement. Would you believe – additional charges from that hotel we never stayed in!'

'So I called, didn't I, Jerry, I called the hotel and they hadn't been closed at all. No renovations, nothing. In fact, our room had been sub-rented that night, to complete strangers, and they'd run up a terrible bill on room service. I tried to explain, but no one wanted to listen.'

'So what did you do?'

Jerry shrugged. 'We paid.'

Whenever they told this story to their friends, Jerry ended up thinking about the stranger's kidney in his body. Most days he never thought about it at all. But somehow it gave him the same feeling that he'd had in Egypt. As if he'd been transplanted, put down somewhere different, and somehow had to keep going.

The Breach

I had never felt such peace. The gentle sway of the cruise ship upon the Norwegian channels created a mesmerizing effect; with my eyes closed, I could imagine myself in a realm of clouds, or else floating, without body, in the dark, star-ridden void. My earbuds encapsulated me in the sounds of sitar and soft Indian chanting. I began to lose myself. The void, the music, the beautiful Nordic scenery that I unconsciously knew was floating by - all this helped to provide the most relaxing setting for meditation.

  It was early March and my vacation along the Norwegian fjords had only just begun. A few nights spent in the mildly bustling heart of Oslo and then I was off, off on the tranquil journey I had so long saved for. Now there was nothing to do but enjoy the peace and quiet. The jangling sitar in the earbuds gradually faded to the sounds of water softly splashing. The water sound gained momentum and began to roar. My meditation became so deep that I began to drift towards sleep. I sunk deeper and deeper, eventually into a dream. My dreams took me to unimagined places. I saw an island in the distance, surrounded by pirate ships en masse, flying flags of an unknown, confederate nation. In my mind's eye I saw sandcastles of unimaginable height crumble, become tortoise shells, and return to the sea, where a mermaid scooped them to her ample bosom. I dreamt strangely, deep and long, of the old gods and their cohorts who ruled the sea long before maps had charted them.

    Suddenly, I was jarred rudely awake. I woke with a gasp and clutched the side of my head, which smarted sharply. My hand came away covered in blood. I was disoriented; I couldn't fathom what had happened. Here I was, meditating and dreaming, when suddenly I was woken, bleeding as if I had been assaulted by one of the weird creatures of my dream-reverie. I was laying on the floor and my clothes were soaking wet. I pulled myself up by hugging the side of the bed, still unbalanced from the wound I had received to the head, and tried desperately to get my bearings. Water seeped steadily in from the cracks between door and hallway. I made my way to the door and jerkily threw it wide, alarm now starting to inhibit basic motor skills.

Water gushed down the hallway in a way I can only describe as wild. It was like the scene from a disaster film; the overhead alarms sounded and cast everything red. The overhead lights flickered, some blown out completely. The sound of the water rushing through the ship was immense; it flooded my senses, its thunderous roar recalling the same sound that I had just a short time ago meditating upon – that had swept me away to the land of dreams.

Using the molding on the walls as purchase, I began to make my way down the hall and towards the nearest emergency exit that I knew of. Struggling against the current, I began to become faint, the strength leaving my body the longer I prodded along. I was almost given out when I finally came upon the steep stairs that led up to the exit. But I was not the only one who had made their way to this spot, as a long line of passengers were halted on and around the steps, nobody moving, only grumbling and cursing their luck. Many wore life-vests already, which reassured me, and I began to look around for some crew member in order to secure my own. There were none to be found. This vast throng of people were all fellow passengers, ranging from small children to the advanced elderly who had wished to look upon the beautiful fjords before they died. The ship began to vibrate in a violent manner, causing a wave of hysteria to work its way through us, as some fell into the churning water and others braced themselves as best they could. I took a young girl by the hand so that she would not slip and tried to give her a reassuring look, though whatever she saw in my eyes only made her begin to cry and beg for her mother.

 Ever so slightly, I began to feel the ship roll to its side. It was tipping; this was it. I was experiencing the kind of capsize that one only reads about. My heart began to pound and I was afraid I squeezed the little girl's hand so hard that her cry became a pitched, anxious scream. Just when I thought all was lost, I saw the crew approaching us from the opposite direction wearing red vests, making their way against the frothing current. The lurid red light of the overheard alarms washed over them in rounds and they seemed to come towards us at a snail's pace. When they were within shouting distance, I heard one of the leading crewmen scream, "There are no more lifeboats. They are all gone!

You must jump! Into the ocean with you all! It is your only chance!"

What followed his announcement was utter pandemonium. Parents and children alike began to wail. Even the elderly, who were previously stoic and composed, started to cry, to curse Jesus and Poseidon alike. At some point I lost the girl. I began to push others aside and struggle towards the steps, which was no easy feat given that most were frozen and weighted down by fright, unable to muster the awareness to make way. It was like wading through a crowd of sleeping buffalo. When I eventually reached the top of the stairs I looked out upon dark waters, the near frozen straights of the Norwegian fjords. Let me tell you: I could *see* the cold. I gazed into those steel grey depths and doubted my courage to do it - to take the final plunge.

"Jump, damn you!", I heard someone shout from behind me. Without turning, I began to make my way closer to the edge.

"Jump you damn fool, or I will throw you overboard myself!"

Still I could not. Hesitantly, I began to retrace my steps. Suddenly I felt someone's hand press against the small of my back and I was pushed violently off and into the water.

The last thing I remember was striking the water. It was blinding cold. I gasped in spite of myself and my lungs filled with ice. And then, complete darkness.

All was dark. I drifted in a sea of black, in a place seemingly without current. I did not know if I was up or down, which way was which. Nothing seemed to matter at that point. I rolled in the afterlife, the nothing that is nonexistence. But to my surprise I soon spied distant lights, like strange willow-the-wisps which flitted about in these blank depths. What could it possibly be? I began to feel the bubbling of consciousness and I willed myself towards them, not swimming, but harnessing a kind of locomotion which simply carried me along.

These luminous spots were not willow-the-wisps at all, nor any other strange creature out of a fairy tale. They were lamps, and they illuminated an underground city of shell and coral. Stalagmites soared upwards from the ocean floor in myriad colors, and around them twisted vague spirits – bearded men, nymphs, ghostly sea-sprites. They beckoned me…forever onward…

I was drawing closer. They were the sea god's couriers, guards, and statesmen. And I belonged to their kingdom.

"She is waking up. Oh god, she made it."

I heard the voice as if from a great distance. I opened my eyes and looked about wildly, expecting to be surrounded by those strange denizens of the fjord's bottom. Only they were ordinary people. They were my fellow passengers, gathered and looking down at me. I recognized the interior of my cabin. There was the Degas, the one of the Parisian milliners; The fire extinguisher attached to the wall.

"Wow, she was really out cold. Are you ok, miss? You must have bumped your head," said an elderly woman as she reached to feel my forehead. "You are bleeding."

A miracle had occurred. I gingerly peeked under my shirt and saw that my bra now consisted of two small tortoise shells, held together by rough twine. I noticed that my hands were somewhat webbed. I wiggled my toes. I had been chosen, had I not?

I'm coming Father. I'm coming Poseidon.
I shouldered my way through the concerned crowd and made for the emergency exit.

A Cruel Odyssey

When I brought up the possibility of early retirement, Barry, my husband, was skeptical.

"No way," he said, "what about Owen's college? The mortgage?"

I reminded him that Owen's college fund was fine and that our mortgage was very nearly paid off in its entirety. We'd worked hard and we'd done well.

"Besides," I said, "I'm too old to be taking calls, cooped up beneath those fluorescent lights all day." I'd been working in the emergency room at the local hospital for nearly three decades and I was ready to get some fresh air, go places I'd never been, see places I couldn't imagine. Barry had already retired from a highly coveted biomedical engineering position a couple years prior, and I was, well, *jealous*. I wanted free time, too, while I was still young enough to enjoy it!

I showed him the pamphlet for a cruise to the

Amazon.

"Imagine all the exotic birds you'll see," I told him, knowing how much he loved birds.

"Plus, Owen needs to be exposed to other places. It's not healthy for a sixteen-year-old boy to just hide up in his room all day. He doesn't seem to have any interests. It worries me, Barry."

Several months later, we found ourselves aboard the *Tranquility,* a gorgeous expedition ship of humble size, boasting completely modern amenities, ample windows and a gleaming deck from which to admire the surrounding ocean as we watched for dolphins or the humps of whales. It was a rather small vessel, relatively speaking, with a capacity for approximately 250 people. We learned that the *Tranquility* had traveled extensively around the world, including to Norway, even to the Antarctic. It was fascinating to stand aboard a boat that had touched cold Arctic waters.

Late one afternoon, Owen came rushing into our cabin.

"We can see land!" He cried, more excited than I'd seen him in a long time. It was a relief to see the boy in a good mood after all that sulking that he did these days.

Barry and I quickly followed Owen to the upper deck. After days on the open water, we could finally see land looming in the not-so-far distance. There was a jittery, excited vibe about the rest of the passengers as we watched the land grow nearer, watched as the luscious mouth of the Amazon River emerged into view.

As the ship sailed onward, the deep blue of the Atlantic Ocean converged with the calm, brownish muddy waters of the Amazon. My excitement was mounting — we'd finally made it! How many people get to have such an amazing opportunity?

Owen had taken to a twenty-something photographer on board called Freddy Powers, who'd been assigned to our dinner table in the evenings. Freddy seemed impressed with Owen's enthusiasm for learning about photography, even letting him borrow a small camera. The two of them couldn't wait to photograph the enchanting sunsets and spectacular scenery that the Amazon cruise would afford us. I felt an inkling of hope: perhaps Owen might take up a new interest, after all?

We befriended the others assigned to our dinner table as well: An older couple from France, plus a pair of young newly-weds from Montana, who'd chosen this adventure for their honeymoon.

Alyssa, the Montana wife, was recalling some fairly scandalous details about their wedding night that made me want to cover Owen's ears when the ship's intercom came on unexpectedly.

"I regret to announce," came the slightly accented voice of our captain, "that we will be skipping our first port of call tomorrow, for security reasons. I apologize for any inconvenience."

"Damn," said Freddy, "I was looking forward to photographing the riverside market —" and he went on to explain to Owen some of the things he'd learned about the locale prior to the trip.

"Security reasons?" Said Barry, turning toward me, "what does that mean?"

"I'm sure there's nothing to worry about," said the French woman, Sabine.

A chill ran down my spine. I just hoped she was right.

So as the *Tranquility* continued upstream, life on board the ship went on. In the evenings we sipped strange cocktails we'd never heard of and we danced late into the night. I even convinced Barry to join in, albeit reluctantly.

"I'm just an engineer!" He kept saying, as if that explained his lack of dancing prowess, "All I do is crunch numbers!" But no one cared, because we were all having too much fun to analyze each other's dancing skills (or lack thereof.)

Yet still, the boat did not stop.

"I thought we were supposed to get off the boat and go on excursions and stuff?" Owen complained over breakfast. He wanted new things to take pictures of with Freddy's camera.

I decided to go ask the captain for information, but no one seemed to know where he was.

That afternoon, a voice came over the intercom to inform us that the ship would be taking a reroute through alternative river channels.

"The waters are low because of the dry season," the voice told us, "so the piers are too high to dock."

As I continued watching from the observatory, slightly hungover from too many Lemon Zingers the night before, the river and shores began to appear dark and mysterious to me, an impenetrable labyrinth.

Like an endless journey we just sailed on. The river channels grew narrower, the *Tranquility* slowed down, and the trees grew yet thicker still.

An air of quiet uncertainty began to befall the passengers. Days before, the sounds of noisy laughter ricocheted from wall-to-wall upon the boat, but that had all wavered to worried whispers.

We're lost, people were saying.

"How can we be lost?" I said to the others over dinner the next day, feeling exasperated by the overactive imagination of the other passengers, "that's nonsense. I think we can trust that the captain knows what he's doing. Goodness knows we paid enough for a decent captain."

But the captain remained unapproachable, keeping his silence. Even the crew members seemed extra agitated, and the servers refused to answer any questions, claiming that everything was fine, that the captain had his reasons. I did not find their reassurances all that convincing, and I began to wonder if the others were right. *Were* we lost?

On the fourth night of seemingly aimless wandering, the whole ship shuddered, awaking me from my uneasy slumber.

"What was that?" I ask, sitting up immediately. Barry was already grabbing his jeans, and he nearly fell over when the ship seemed to jar suddenly to a halt.

I threw on a light shawl and we stepped into the chaos of the hallway. It seemed that the jolt had awoken everyone on board, and passengers were running up and down the hallways in blatant confusion and rising fear. Owen appeared at my side.

"What's going on, Mom?" He asked, trying to sound nonchalant, but I could tell he was afraid.

Alyssa and Carter, the Montana newly-weds, materialized toward the end of the hall, waving at us, pushing through the crowd.

"People are getting off the boat," Carter said, breathing heavily, "we don't know what to do."

"Grab your flashlights," said Barry authoritatively, "let's go."

All rooms were equipped with small flashlights in the event of an emergency. Swallowing nervously, I wasn't sure if this constituted as an emergency or not, but it certainly felt like one.

It appeared that several passengers had already climbed overboard and we could see the bobbing of their flashlights along the riverbank. Except for flurried whispers, the ship was silent, and lights were out.

"Where's the captain?" Alyssa whispered, clutching Carter's elbow.

"Everything's going to be okay," I said, hoping that Alyssa couldn't hear my voice shake. The reality was, we had no idea where the nearest port of call was, and I didn't want to think about what creatures we might stumble upon, traipsing about in the jungle in the middle of the night. Weren't there tigers out there?

"Why are passengers leaving the boat?" Barry said.

"It's not the passengers," said Freddy, showing up behind us, "it's the crew."

"The *crew?*"

I watched, panic-stricken, as the people walking along the riverbank seemed to disappear into the density of the forest.

No one could sleep after hearing about being abandoned by the crew. We paced back and forth on the deck, along with dozens of other passengers.

Then, rustling could be heard along the riverbank, and as some of us shined our lights downward, I thought I could make out several figures below.

"Barry," I whispered, "I think there's people down there. Maybe the crew is coming back."

And as we looked, we realized that that were, indeed, people walking along the riverbank. I squinted against the darkness, watching as they stepped into the moonlight.

I gasped. They were not the crew members at all, but oddly dressed strangers. With machetes. And guns. Suddenly, they begin to start climbing aboard.

People were panicking now, and I stepped away from the railing, holding onto my husband and son. Some brave soul called out a question to the newcomers, but the men responded in a language that wasn't English at all.

"Let's go," I said quickly, pulling my family away, "we need to get back to the cabin."

We started to move hurriedly back inside, but not before I glanced back to see three of these strangers already upon the boat, frisking a passenger.

We broke into a run, many of us crowding into the

hallway at once, trying to push through each other to the safety of our rooms.

Finally, we were able to shove our way into our cabin.

I locked the door behind us.

Suddenly, a scream burst out somewhere in the hallway. A crashing, splintering sound erupted into the night, the sound of doors being kicked in.

Fearfully, I took Barry's and Owen's hands into mine and we huddled in the corner of the room, beside the bed. As an afterthought, Barry jumped to his feet to grab the three-legged stool that sat before the vanity table, presumably to use as a weapon if necessary.

You're just an engineer, I thought.

The noise of a woman and child crying reached my ears, and the sounds of a scuffle floated into the room. A fight had broken out.

A gunshot.

And then, silence. After endless hours of sitting there, a trickle of morning light peaked through the window, and Barry — still clutching the stool as a weapon — went out into the hall to investigate.

"They're gone," he said upon his return, and I felt like I could breathe again.

A noise growing in the distance one again drew the passengers to the deck. Within minutes, the boat was being swarmed by what appeared to be military patrol boats. My first inclination was to retreat back to my cabin, but Barry stopped me.

"I think they're here to rescue us!" He said.
Soon they were boarding the ship, and we were asked to retrieve our things.

We were going home.

Our cruel odyssey came to an end in Macapá, Brazil. We bid farewell to our new friends, and, after signing some mandatory paperwork, boarded our flight to Fort Lauderdale so that we could finally return to the peace of our own home.

Weeks later, it was Freddy Powers who contacted us with the news.

"Did you hear?" He asked, "the *Tranquility* captain got arrested in Venezuela, along with some of the other crew members. He wasn't even the real captain. The real captain was kidnapped before we even boarded in Trinidad. It was all planned from the beginning."

When I hung up, Barry was grinning.

"So where are we going next?" He asked.

The Casino

The *MS Spell of the Seas* churned through the Caribbean as I made my way into the larger of its two casinos. The sharp tang of sea air faded away as I entered, greeted by bright lights and a cacophony of voices. I took a deep breath of the over-oxygenated air. This was exactly what I was looking for.

My name is James. I've spent the latter half of my 41 years spending a generous inheritance however I wanted, and in the last ten or so I've discovered the joy of cruise ship casinos. Cruise ships have two things over Vegas – free food and free entertainment. It makes up for having to buy your own drinks, though I've not been much of a drinker since my partying days in my 30's. Gambling is more fun with a clear head – the thrill of a win, the enticing promise of a loss, the moment when the cards flip and the numbers could add up to anything

The *Spell* was well known as a top of the line cruise ship, its white fiberglass sides adorned with its name in elegant letters. It was a large ship with several hundred cabins, three restaurants, a bar, and its two casinos. I was only interested in the latter.

    I picked an hors d'voeures from a waiter's platter and popped it in my mouth as I glanced over the room. A stage in the center featured a woman in black crooning an old ballad, and surrounding her were the usual table games. Craps, roulette, blackjack, and in the corner even a game of Pai Gow. Along the wall was a row of slot machines. They looked like the perfect way to whet my appetite for dinner later.

    I sat at the machines, playing it safe with small denominations, and scanned the room. People watching was as much a part of the casino experience as gambling – it could even be more entertaining than the entertainment itself. I watched an elderly man trade his chips for drinks every time he won at roulette. A young couple hovered over the craps table, throwing their hands up in the air and cheering at each win. After I had a few losses, I shrugged and pocketed the rest of my money. There were other games to play.

    I came back each night, wandering from one game to the next, always drawn eventually to the slots where I would sit and lose until I couldn't take it anymore.

    On the third night, after more losses, I stood and surveyed the room. Among the shouts and dinging of the occasional win, something had caught my attention. Down the line of slots sat a beautiful Caribbean woman with dark hair and eyes. She wore an elegant red dress that hugged her thick curves, but what grabbed my attention was not her looks. Each time she pulled the slots reel, she won with a giggle and a shout. She had been here the night before as well, winning just as frequently.

A crowd of bystanders ebbed and flowed around her as she won again and again, and I waited for them to dissipate before heading toward her. She looked up as I approached, pausing in her game to smile at me.

"James," I said, by way of introduction, and I held my hand out. "And you are?"

"Marina," she said in a thick accent. Marina smiled and placed her hand in mine and I kissed it with a bow. She giggled just as she had done at each of her slot wins.

"You seem very lucky tonight, Marina." I eyed the slot machine as discreetly as I could, looking for any device or trick that might betray cheating.

"Oh, I am lucky every night here. This machine, it is my lucky machine. I play at this time of night when luck is strongest."

"May I have a try?"

"Of course."

She stood and waved me towards the machine. I sat, then pulled the reel. The slots rolled, and I waited with bated breath – a loss. I rolled again. A loss. With a frustrated snort, I stood.

"It seems the luck has run out," I said, forcing a smile. The ship's clock rang six times as we stared at each other, then she smiled back and sat down, starting another game as she did. The slots rolled and – a win! Not just a win, but the jackpot! Several bystanders clapped as money poured out of the machine.

"Perhaps not." She collected her winnings and left me there, my mouth hanging open. I was pushed out of the way as others crowded around the slots hoping for a win. I went back up to my room, determined to win tomorrow.

I headed to the casino early that morning, while it was still empty. I went straight to the machine where she had won the night before and inspected it again, kneeling to look underneath and even prying it away from the wall to check the back. Nothing seemed out of the ordinary.

I sat down and thought for a moment. I knew from my many years gambling that there was no such thing as luck. A winner would become a loser, given long enough, and anyone who didn't lose was cheating. Something must be special about this machine.

I tried a game and lost. Again. Loss. Again. Loss. I sat at that machine for over an hour without winning once, and finally I threw up my hands and left, my blood boiling. From what she had said, she would be here again tonight, and I would figure out what was going on.

I entered the casino at the same time as last night, scanning the room for Marina – there she was at the same machine, winning a small prize. I began to head over and then thought better of it, backing off to watch from a distance.

An hour went by and she continued to win small change. I couldn't see anything strange about her technique, and I already knew nothing made the machine different than any other machine on the ship. I was furious. Why did she keep winning? The clock tolled six as she played again, and the machine lit up wildly – jackpot! I felt my blood boil and I turned on my heel and left without watching her collect the winnings.

I stopped outside the casino and took a deep breath, trying to calm my anger. An elderly black man stood just under the awning, sipping a drink and watching me with a keen eye. When he did not look away, I headed over to him. I kept it to myself that I was furious.

"Can I help you?" I asked, frowning. He chuckled.

"You're not the only one watching her. I'm a regular, just like her. She wins every night."

"How?"

The old man chuckled again and shook his head.

"Nobody knows. She can only win when the machine is full – that's why she tells suckers like you it's lucky. You pay in hoping for luck, and she cashes out. Truth is, she's the lucky one. No one can win at that machine but her."

"She's cheating; it's obvious. I just have to find out how!"

The old man tilted his head and looked over my shoulder.

"Seems now's your chance."

I whirled around to see Marina headed toward her cabin. I slipped after her, sticking to the shadows as she made her way up to the balcony suites. I watched from behind a corner as she headed down the hall and turned again. I ran after her, but as I rounded the next corner she was gone.

I crept from door to door, listening at each until I came to the end of the hall. A stray bill sat in front of the door, and I picked it up. This must be Marina's room!

I pressed my ear to the door, and as I did so I smelled the sharp scent of an herbal candle. A light shone suddenly from under the door, and I heard faint chanting from within. The chanting gave way to inhuman noises, moans and some kind of demonic chattering. I could see the light flickering under the door, and the candle scent became stronger. Was this some kind of voodoo ritual? Was her luck supernatural?

I heard footsteps approach the door and I backed away. Suddenly my vision went white and I felt like I was falling. My life passed before my eyes as though I was dreaming, and then everything faded to darkness.

When I awoke, I sat among a pile of pillows and blankets, the scent of the candle fading around me. Marina sat across a low table from me, her hands folded in her lap and a strange smile on her face.

"You are brave... or perhaps stupid," she said. Some strange magic compelled me to speak the truth, and I just shook my head.

"There's no such thing as luck. I had to know how you were winning."

"Luck?" she said, her smile widening. "No, I know something stronger. As a reward for your curiosity – would you like to try it?"

I thought hard before I answered. The ability to win every slot roll, as many times as I wanted? What could be better? But I knew there had to be a catch.

"And what will I owe you?"

"Nothing. But the spell will work on this ship only."

After a moment I nodded. She immediately closed her eyes and raised her hands as she began to mumble a quiet chant. I felt the air in the room begin to move, and a candle suddenly burst into flame. Hardly a second later she lowered her hands and opened her eyes.

"I don't feel any different," I said, looking down at my body.

"You will. You will see it, your lucky machine. Trust your instincts."

Without warning, I blacked out again.

The next morning I woke up sure that the previous night had been a dream. I avoided the casino until the evening, unsure what I would find there, but around dinner I finally got up the courage to head over. As I entered, the row of slot machines caught my eye again – one in particular almost felt like it was calling to me. As I walked toward it I noticed Marina at her usual machine. She winked at me as I passed.

I sat down at the machine nervously, and after a moment finally started a game. It rolled and – a win! A small win, but I had a feeling more was to come.

My wins got progressively larger until a crowd gathered around me. I told each of them what Marina had told me – this was my lucky machine, and they should try it. Just before six a young woman in blue came over to me.

"You seem lucky," she said. The clock tolled six and I grinned. I rolled. Jackpot!

"It's all the machine, really," I said as I collected my winnings. I gestured to the seat as I left, and when I glanced over my shoulder the young woman had sat down. I grinned. I would be back tomorrow night.

The Space Cruise

To this day, Ben Iglesias has not been able to explain it. What had really happened? His life was no worse than before. But the strange thing was, that the feeling of not belonging here was not going away. However, that was not important anymore.

It all began with the return flight from a three day space cruise back to earth, a journey which he had planned for a long time. He was actually the only passenger on board, nevertheless for him it was supposed to be a dream vacation for which he paid a substantial part of his savings. Also, for two of the four crew members it was their first trip to space, so due to their relative inexperience there was a small risk to be taken, however he could never have dreamt the outcome of this journey. Ben has never been the same person afterward.

As they entered the earths' orbit, the whole vessel began shaking, a flickering light appeared for a couple of seconds, alarm signals were ringing everywhere. And suddenly he lost consciousness.

When he woke up his crew was dead and the spacecraft was on emergency electricity, but the strangest thing was that the spacecraft had already landed and all the instruments were dead.

It was impossible to see how much time had passed since the accident, it might have been seconds or centuries. The weather, the coordinates, the data of the ship could not be correct. More important was the fact that there was no contact with the base. Everything seemed dead.

For a couple of seconds Ben looked out of the window. Where was the Caribbean Sea? He was supposed to be in Cuba, but under the ship everything was yellow and brown.

Ben exited the spaceship and saw a white desert until the end of the horizon. It was very hot and the atmosphere had only 60% oxygen.

Suddenly, he could not believe what he saw. Slowly but surely, a group of humans approached. They surrounded him and said nothing. Ben was not afraid, because they did not look aggressive, but completely different.

The people were small, they were women and a couple of men and they looked like .... burned? Were they Australian Aborigines? There was some resemblance, but they were very thin, almost like skeletons and small as children. They gave Ben water and signaled him to follow the group. After a long walk they came to a valley of stones, covered with small holes that were entrances to giant dark caves. From somewhere down there came the sound of water.

That was Ben's first impression. How long had he lived here now? Ben estimated that he had already lived with these creatures for about three years. At first, the language was the most difficult part. Now they were like his family. His wife was four heads smaller than him, but it worked. She always smiled at him. Life was no longer important. Ben felt good, his wife had the eyes of a black cat and every day she laughed more, she had become pregnant.

The Ghost Cruise Liner

It had always been a dream of ours to explore the Pacific. It seemed the crown jewel of the world. Just think, the numerous islands that dot that wild expanse, all rife with untold mystery. That's right, even my wife and son shared in this romance; I didn't have to do much convincing to get them to go on this trip. We meant to visit many of the islands in the western Pacific, but we decided to start our journey with a few leisurely days spent in Hawaii. Though conventional and mired in all that is wrong with modern tourism, everything went swell for us there. Yes, everything was fine until we boarded that private jet headed for Saipan. Though I could not point to anything outwardly wrong with the scenario, as I buckled my seatbelt I whispered to my wife that I did not like the look of the Guamanian pilot. I had caught a glimpse of him before he disappeared into the cockpit: aside from his strange, shuffling gait, his uniform befitted the era of silent movies. A strange character indeed.

One hour into the flight the pilot noticed a strange cloud directly below us. He informed us over the intercom that he believed something of gargantuan proportions must be situated under it. My family and I became incredibly curious. I opened the door to the cockpit and begged the captain to take us to a lower altitude so that we could better see what the phenomenon was. As the plane descended, we slowly made out more and more detail. Finally, we were able to make out what the large blotch upon the ocean actually was and were immediately struck dumb: a massive cruise ship that appeared ripped from another century entire, scorched black and partially destroyed, but still floating, as if animated by powers otherworldly. The water around the ship virtually glowed with a strange luminescence, a milky white shot through with tones of green.

The pilot took the plane on several slow circuits around the wreckage so that we could soak up this unusual sight. On closer inspection, we saw motion on the vessel's deck. Something or someone was moving about in rapid, jerking movements. From above they looked like small ants scrambling across the deck's surface. But the harder we strained to make them out, the blurrier they became, if you can imagine that. In my mind's eye I imagined they were people, desperate for our help; they looked up at the sky in wonder at our appearance, and with clasped hands beseeched our pity.

My husband began to do some research on his laptop while the pilot circled the wreckage. He googled the history of shipwrecks in this area of the globe, comparing the wreckage below to the images on the screen.

"Pilot, take us a bit lower so that I can make out that wrecked ship better. I can't quite discern enough details for a real comparison," my husband called in to the cockpit.

The pilot skillfully lowered our altitude until we were only about 100 yards or so above the wreckage. We started to make out the details of the ship more clearly, but still, the little "ants" that raced about its deck remained a blur, like motes tickling the edge of one's vision. As we drew closer, everyone realized there was something *off* about this ship. It looked like the Titanic, or else some ship out of a 19th century storybook, tricked out with antique steam stacks, rigging, and the like.

My husband suddenly gasped. "It cannot be," he said, "all things considered that wrecked ship there is the Kichi Maro! Or else it is the museum replica! Look at this picture."

I simply couldn't believe it. It *was* the Kichi Maro, the Japanese cruise liner that sank during a typhoon on the 22nd of September 1912.

It was a disaster that had claimed more than 1,000 lives, though it had been overshadowed by the tragic events of the Titanic.

Our immediate concern, aside from the delirious wonder we felt at finding a ship afloat that should have been resting at the bottom of the sea for at least a century, was the strange creatures crawling across the ship's deck.

"They could be seals," I said to my husband.

"Honey, have you ever seen seals move like that? They flit hither and thither like a pack of spirits. It is uncanny!"

"Pilot, can you get us any closer without risking our safety? No, ok…I think I can make out one of those things. It has two arms … no, I can't really say…"

"Let's take some pictures. We can get them developed and later magnified. Then we may be able to make them out better," I said. "This is the discovery of the century! Just think, the Kichi Maro, surfaced and nearly whole!"

A couple hours later we landed in Saipan without more ado. We had the pictures developed at the local supermarket and we eagerly poured over them once back at our motel. But lo and behold, they were all blank. Not only did they show nothing of the ship or the strange denizens we were so curious about, but they were utterly white. Like we had taken photographs of a blank, featureless wall.

Six months later we held a gathering of select friends in order to tell them of our strange discovery. We related the circumstances surrounding the infamous Japanese cruise liner and showed them the photographs that had all come back mute and white. They immediately heard the truth in our words and wanted to investigate this scene for themselves. We agreed to travel to the location by boat in order to get a closer look at the wreckage.

We rented a large sailing yacht in Guam and made it directly for the spot, as my husband had saved the coordinates from the previous occasion. We were nearly there when a violent storm suddenly overcame us; it felt and looked like a typhoon! The yacht was equipped with all the modern radio and transmission devices you'd expect, but we were still caught completely unaware. It had not even appeared as a blip on the satellite image. It seemed to have developed out of thin air, which was virtually impossible.

Just when we thought all was lost, with the waves lashing us about and the wind reaching a horrific crescendo, we entered a place of strange calm, like an oasis in the wild, belligerent waters. We had evidently crossed into the eye of the typhoon, and what do you know, there she was: the magnificent, decadent Kichi Maro.

"See! I told you!" I shouted to our friends. They all looked at the gigantic wreck in dismay. It loomed over us, in all its broken glory. We drew closer and discovered that the ship was covered in vast scars, black swaths that looked like the result of fire. Large parts of the ship were covered in broken coral, a sickly brand of grey invertebrate that wrapped itself around the ship like a monstrous python. All the chimneys were missing; the blown-out windows gaped at us ominously.

We saw the creatures moving again as we got closer to the ship, but try as we did, we could make out nothing more than blurs. A few of us snapped photographs. When we were only a hand's width away, I reached out and touched the great grey hull. It was pulsing and vaguely warm. I looked up and noticed dark clouds closing in and urged my husband to steer us away. The storm began to rage around us again, and the water became nearly as choppy as before. But strangely enough, directly in front of our yacht, the way was clear and placid. It was like a strange force guided us through the storm, making way for the yacht. Soon we were back upon untroubled waters.

We never talked much about that experience. None of us did. It had chilled us to the bone and forced a pact of silence upon us. The crew split up after we anchored, all going their separate ways, back to a world that thereafter made less sense.

The pictures I developed were again, as you can probably already guess, entirely blank.

High Waves

I've been single a long time. I'd like to say it's not because of my looks; in fact, I *know* it's not because of my looks. I'm an attractive woman in my mid-thirties, and I could have just about any young bachelor I want. I see the way men look at me. With my lustrous brown hair and long legs, which retain their youthful tone from regular exercise, it's no wonder. No, the reason I am still single is because I'm picky, and by nature very reserved. It takes a lot to get to know me, but once you do, I'm a friend for life. That's why I thought it would be a good thing to go on a cruise. Virtually everyone onboard are strangers, and with no history or emotional baggage to worry about, I thought I would be able to meet some new people, maybe even a man my own age. That was my thinking at least; what happened on the cruise kind of turned everything upside down.

I booked a cruise that would take me around the Mediterranean, and the brochure showed pictures of all the charming little towns and ports that the ship would visit. I was looking forward to visiting all these secluded spots I knew of only through hearsay. It sounded perfect. Additionally, it departed from Barcelona, which is not far from where I live. Nothing unusual happened until the night we boarded. I mean, otherwise I wouldn't be writing this account now – it's just a cruise for Pete's sake. See, that night, staff announced that they had taken a large group of refugees on board. I'm pretty liberal, and I think we should help when help is needed, but this was unprecedented. After all, this was a luxury cruise liner. Every passenger paid a pretty penny for this trip. Why would we take on refugees?

Anyway, I didn't see a single refugee during the first few days of the voyage. Hey, out of sight, out of mind. I was enjoying myself, though the weather could have been better. There were often sudden storms, and one had to be mindful when sunbathing because it could just start raining out of nowhere. But for the most part it was pleasant. I liked the food, and all the curious activities planned for the guests. I even made a few friends. But my pleasure turned to concern on our 5th day out from port. We were making for the French Riviera when the weather took a turn and stayed that way. Great storms assailed us, and the water grew incredibly turbulent. The staff cautioned us to stay in our cabins and hunker down.

I think the next thing that happened shocked everyone on the boat pretty bad, for there was an alert voiced over the intercom system that one of the ship's engines had failed. I soon became ill on account of the ship pitching about, and I heard others through the paper-thin walls vomiting and moaning. The funny thing is, right about this time, I could hear someone having a riotous party. Well, at least *someone* was enjoying themselves.

Suddenly, the lights in my cabin shut off. I was reaching for my phone when a voice again came over the intercom. They said the ship was in a state of emergency and on lockdown. We were strictly forbidden to leave our cabins. I was starting to panic, and the siren from the hallway only made matters worse, for it made danger that much more apparent.

Then there was a knock on my door, strangely enough. I thought it was probably some official to calm me down and explain matters further. When I cracked the door, the hall was nearly dark, but I could make out a series of dark faces by the ghastly red luminescence of the alarm system. It was a family of refugees.

"Hello? Can I help you with something?"

The father of the family looked at me with a serene, childlike expression before asking if he and his family could take refuge in my cabin until the storm abated. I didn't know what else to say, so I invited them in as warmly as I could, given the circumstances.

"Sure…come in. Yes, this is terrible. I don't know what is happening either."

I soon learned that they were a family from The Gambia, and they had only recently arrived in Spain. Besides the husband and wife, there were two small children, hardly more than toddlers, and a lad of about sixteen, if I had to guess.

I became quick friends with the mother, who had a gentle way about her. We talked at length, trying to block out all the carnage of the storm.

"See miss, we were not welcome in Spain. The authorities told us that we had to leave; that they had no more room for migrants like us."

"I'm so sorry to hear that," I said to her in return. "I wish people would be more understanding nowadays. Everyone needs a place to live peacefully."

"Yes, that's why we smuggled ourselves onto this boat. My husband thought it was better to try our luck in France, or maybe Greece. Maybe there they will be more welcoming…but I don't know."

"What else can you do? Really, you can stay here with me until we reach the mainland. Just in case the staff comes snooping about."

We talked long into the night, while the husband played cards with his children, and the sixteen-year-old shyly looked at me out of the corner of his eye while he pretended to be occupied with his phone. Truth be told, I was embarrassed to meet his eye as well. He was gorgeous, with princely features and a body to match, but I knew I was much too old for him. What could possibly come of such a thing?

I helped prepare bedding for the family to sleep on. Sometime later, when I thought everyone fast asleep, I felt a hand grope for me in the dark. I lay completely still, thinking it must have been my imagination. But no, it was the young boy, and he was sliding into bed with me. I let his hands clumsily explore my body, as I did not know what else to do at the time. I really didn't want to cause a scene, and I thought if I just feigned sleep, he would eventually leave me alone. His parents were sleeping not three yards away; there was no chance in hell he would try to rape me or do anything unseemly. Right when I was thinking this, he slid his hand under the waistband of my pajamas. I gasped and stifled an urge to scream.

    Not five seconds later, the lights in the cabin came back on. They must have gotten the power generator operating again, just in time. I sat up and looked about.

The boy was huddled in a corner, looking more terrified than I was.

When I went to report the incident, I could find no one to help me, since everyone was preoccupied with getting the ship righted. A hysterical woman with vague claims about rape was not exactly first on their list of priorities.

Eventually, some two weeks later, the ship made its last port of call. I breathed an inward sigh of relief. Not only would I finally rid myself of the refugee family, who, though pleasant, were all starting to wear on my nerves, but I could finally make an official report concerning my ordeal with the young man, Fernando.

Alas, when I filed the report, the police took me seriously, but they could find no evidence of any refugees having been on board the cruiser. I gave them detailed descriptions, but to no avail; it seemed that the refugee family had hightailed it off the ship as soon as we docked. As they were "stowaways", the police could find no records of them. I simply had to give up and take it on the chin.

A year later, on a quiet Monday afternoon, I received a letter with a return address from The Gambia. It was a love letter, elegantly written. Never had I read such a description of emotion, such poetry.

The next day I booked airline tickets to Banjul, The Gambia. In the letter he described it as an *unforgettable night. One for the* ages. No longer did I want to report and incriminate young Fernando. The opposite had occurred: where there was once resentment, I now found longing and lust. That night with Fernando, despite all my misgivings, I'd felt *alive*. I'm writing this as I fly to The Gambia. It is my testament, an ode to our strange, forbidden love.

The Cherry Blossom Stones

My husband and I have always been adventure-minded people. In fact, that's really the reason we first decided to start dating. I still remember our first encounter, and the twinkle which showed in his eyes when I said my real passion was to *explore*. Now, when I say "explore", I don't mean the forays reserved for the bourgeoisie, but the good, honest, off-the-beaten-track kind. That's why when we began to plan our honeymoon together, we considered long and hard which mysterious country we'd like to visit most. We ended up settling on Japan, given the airy mists which seem to hang about that land in one's imagination, and we were not disappointed in our choice. You will soon see why.

    We thought the best way to really see and explore Japan was by cruise ship. Plus, we would have all the added benefits that a cruise liner has to provide: the unlimited food and alcohol, heated pools, and social activities. It really was like killing two birds with one stone. Japan also held a special allure for my husband, for he is an avid collector of precious stones. Since he was a little boy, he has hoarded stones bought and found, from the simple purple quartz to the more exclusive forms of fossils which formed the cream of the crop of his collection. He now sells and trades in precious stones and minerals, a side occupation which is fruitful enough to pay for excursions like the one we were presently on. There was one stone in particular that my husband had always sought, and that was the "cherry blossom stone", native to Japan. It is said that they are typically found embedded in hornfels, whose metamorphic process aids in the cherry blossom's development. These stones are *only* found in the caves of Honshu Island, off the coast of southern Japan. Now you start to see why my husband pinned so much for a honeymoon cruising these straits.

Fortunately, our ship was scheduled to dock at Himeji port, and we knew that there were supposedly caves rich in cherry blossom stones thereabouts, as long as one was able to find a guide willing to take a foreigner into these sacred regions. With a little bit of persistence and pestering of the locals, we were given directions to a man who might be able to lead us to one of the caves. He lived in a little fishing shack on the edge of town, and when we approached his abode, we saw smoke rising from the chimney into the crisp morning air. We knocked several times before a shrunken, crabby old man opened the front door, wearing a kasa and blinking at us sheepishly.

"Good sir," said my husband, "we were told that you may, if given sufficient payment, guide us to the caves where lie the famous cherry blossom stones?"

At first, I was sure that he did not speak nor understand English, as he just stared at my husband with a sour expression. But after several moments, he answered him in heavily accented English.

"I do. I do. But…"

"Yes? I'm a collector. I also have a lot of cash." My husband proceeded to flash him a fistful of Japanese yen.

"Ah, I see," said the little old man. It seemed decided. Little else was spoken between us before setting off.

The cave mouth he led us to was yawning and dark, so dark that our eyes could not discern much past several yards. To get there the guide led us through a ravine and across a valley, through forest and over field alike, and we became disoriented. We did not even know which direction the port of Himeji now lay. If it were not for our sure-footed guide, we would have been quite beside ourselves, even though we likened ourselves "explorers". That said, we were admittedly hesitant to enter the cave mouth. It looked so foreboding. But our little guide reassured us with kind words.

"Don't worry. Mr. Akira see you through. It not be so dark. I have electric lantern."

With the help of Mr. Akira's lantern, we slowly made our way into the cave and started to explore its depths. It seemed that it had no end, and as we got deeper into its warrens, we noticed that a thick moisture clung to the walls, slimy and faintly luminescent. We asked our guide about this, but he was strangely silent on the matter. He brought up our rear, holding the lantern aloft while my husband chose which passage to take. Suddenly my husband stopped and said that he thought we must turn around; this was evidently not the way to the hoard of stones. It was then that the cave was thrown into utter darkness. It was like all life had been snuffed out. We called out for Mr. Akira, but he did not respond.

"What in the hell. Was this some kind of hoax? Where did he go?"

My husband groped for me in the dark.

"I have my cell phone. Hold on, I can use the flashlight app," I said reassuringly.

We could see now, though somewhat sparingly. The weak light of the phone only illuminated what was directly in front of us. Nevertheless, there was no sign of our guide, Mr. Akira. It was like he had suddenly vanished into thin air.

"What are we going to do now? We only have a little over 6 hours before we need to be back at the ship". At this point I wanted my husband to take control.

"I don't know. Let's try to backtrack while we still have light from your phone. Otherwise we are doomed."

We were terribly scared, verging on panic. I could hear my husband's ragged breathing in front of me. He seemed to be picking directions at random, becoming more and more desperate.

When all seemed lost, we entered a chamber that was bathed in golden light. There were stones and crystals everywhere, of all sizes and dimensions, specimens that were worth small fortunes. My husband said he couldn't believe it; he was quite lost for words. It was like coming to the end of the rainbow and discovering the mythic pot of gold. Alas, I told my husband we couldn't linger; my phone's battery was almost dead. He had begun to fill his pockets, choosing stones he deemed most exemplary. I snapped a few photographs before my husband told me not to waste any more of the battery.

"Please, honey, just fill your pockets with stones. Don't worry about pictures. We are rich!"

Now burdened by our load, we left the chamber on its opposite end, following the repeated sound of what we thought was a great gong being rung. This "gong" became clearer as we continued in this direction, and we eventually found a tunnel with daylight at the end. We had made it.

When we got back to civilization, it was difficult to find a taxi to take us to the port, as nobody seemed to understand a lick of English. We finally convinced a shady looking fellow in an unmarked car to take us back to the ship, but he demanded an exuberant amount of money once we were parked at the dock.

"I'm sorry…I have no more money. But, well, I do have…these rocks."

My husband prodded me to show him a few examples from my pockets. The driver, who omitted an air of electric violence, snatched them out of my hand and scrutinized them.

"Give them to me. All of them. Or I kill you."

Needless to say, we gave him most of our findings. We hightailed it out of there and onto our ship before he could demand more. At least my husband got to keep a few of his favorite samples. Though we didn't have much to show for when we eventually arrived back home, the few photos I took attested to our marvelous discovery. On social media it became known as "The Cave of Delights", and we are now known as that *daring* couple, explorers of the first order. We may not have gotten rich, but at least we are famous.

A Special Cooking Course

My wife and I spent last year on one of the new cruise lines around the southern half of Japan. It was upon the Merry Princess, a 2,500-passenger behemoth that contained every luxury and distraction that a modern man could possibly crave. We both found it to be a relaxing, easy and relatively inexpensive way to explore some of the more "off-the-beaten-path" areas of the country. We were having a grand time, and we both experienced the peace of mind that comes from untethering yourself from the troubles of daily life. That is why I was so shocked to one day wake up and find myself in a hospital bed. It was certainly not the way I had envisioned ending our cruise.

Anyway, we stopped in Beppu, a spa town designed for tourists and built over an active geothermal area. This feature afforded the town nine small clusters of hot springs and geysers known, somewhat cheekily, as

"The Hells". English was not widely spoken here and the signs about the town were just an indiscernible jumble of Japanese kanji. It left us a little disoriented, but is disorientation not the pleasure of the real tourist? To find oneself without bearings, that is the mark of true adventure, or at least that is what I tried to tell myself at the time. We dipped our toes into the culture without putting our *entire* foot in, and I think we were all the happier for it. We saw and experienced some really authentic things. My wife already knew a little about the local culture, so she helped me when I was most ill at ease.

    One of the activities we chose was a cooking course conducted in one of the many beautiful parks around Beppu. I already knew a thing or two about Japanese cooking and cuisine, but I was far from being a pro. I've never been a fan of sushi nor shabu-shabu, and I generally prefer my Asian food to be of the shopping mall variety. But I wanted to humor my wife so I agreed to take part in the course. The instructor was an elderly man who was so short that he had to stand on a box to see over the "etsubin", a Japanese term for a cast iron kettle used for boiling water. This one in front of him was huge, nearly a yard across and heated from hot stones pulled from the nearby springs. To our disgust, he threw living frogs into the open kettle, where they crashed into the water with a great *hiss* and sizzle.

Frogs have always been one of my favorite animals, and I treat them with a kind of reverence they may not even deserve. But I felt that I had to protest this cruel behavior. I stepped forward and shouted at him like a drunken sailor, loud and obnoxiously so that he would surely get my message. I probably looked like a real madman.

"Hey man, what do you think you are doing!? At least kill those frogs in a humane way. Don't just toss them into boiling water like their lives are of so little value!"

My wife pulled me aside and explained to me that one of the rules of this culture was never to disagree with your elders in a public setting, such as a meeting or a group course like the one we were partaking in. She told me that I was doing the instructor a grave disservice and that I was causing him to "lose face", something they call "mentsu wo ushinau". I looked at the little old man and saw him scowling at me, his face turning a deep purple under his kasa.

But this did not matter to me at the time. I was so taken aback by his treatment of the frogs that I was blinded by rage; all custom and delicacy was thrown to the wind. This would simply not be tolerated. I pointed my finger at him and explained that animal cruelty was something I simply could not let go.

"End this show right now! This…this…spectacle!"

I was nearly slobbering with rage. He came forward and jabbed a gnarled, crooked finger into my chest and told me that "we are still in Japanese territory" or something of the like. I couldn't quite make out what he said; he mumbled in a strange, rasping dialect. My wife then whispered into my ear that he had challenged me to show how frogs can be cooked without harming them. He wanted me to show the audience a real alternative to the process he adhered to. I saw him standing there, now with a smug smile spreading across his face, motioning me towards the box where he had been presiding over the boiling cauldron.

"Go on. Show me how to properly cook these frogs young man". He gestured again.

I suddenly became unsure of myself. I had never cooked frogs in my life. But I decided to show some courage and approached the wooden platform. I would end this spectacle on my own terms. The people around us, the tourists and growing crowd of locals alike, applauded, curiosity plainly written on their faces. When I stepped up onto the box and looked out onto the crowd, I was quite at a loss about what to do. I didn't have the heart to kill these frogs, no matter the method. Could I just swiftly chop their heads off? That was unthinkable. I could think of no other means except…throwing them into the boiling water. In the end, I decided that the best course of action was just to take the bag with the frogs away. I could disappear into some alley and let them go there. That way, they could live a happy life amongst the puddles and rotten drainage. At least I would end this cruel charade!

I started to gather all the frogs and place them tenderly in the bag, for I did not want to crush any of them in my haste. I was muttering things under my breath, like "this will show him", or "this is how a civilized man acts". Done handling the frogs, I started to turn, for I was about to make a break for it, when I was suddenly pushed from behind. He must have realized what I planned to do. I fell forward and before I knew it, my entire being was awash in blinding pain. Heat enveloped me; I felt it sear my bones. I passed out.

When I came to, I was in the hospital that I mentioned at the beginning of this tale. The sterile surroundings confused me; I was awash in hard, white light. I quickly noticed that my legs and feet were wrapped entirely in bandages. I looked at my arms: the surface of my skin looked like dirty, pinkish crushed stone, or a kind of oddly cured leather sometimes found on antique saddles, left in the sun far too long.

Later, the Japanese doctor teasingly scolded me. It seemed he had gotten wind of what had really occurred in the park. As he was taking my temperature he looked down with a merry twinkle in his eye and said, "Hey, this is what you get for causing someone to lose face. It could have gone even worse for you. Us Japanese are forgiving folk. You have only been boiled alive."

Bermuda Marriage

The first time I laid eyes on Harry I had a feeling he was the one. He was lounging on one of the poolside chairs, wearing a little mint green speedo and a pair of designer sunglasses. My, was he handsome. I was instantly smitten, and after making his acquaintance, I learned that we shared many of the same interests and desires. First and foremost, he loved to go on cruises. Second, he loved adventure, and as everyone knows, adventure can readily be found lurking around every corner of every port town around Bermuda. Now, I'm just a penny-pinching nobody, but I like to think I have an adventurer's soul, no matter how dormant it may seem at times. I'm also a little overweight, with a slight limp inherited from a childhood surgical procedure gone awry, but I like to think I'm somewhat attractive, nonetheless. Men have always told me that I'm "cute". Harry, a self-made businessman from Canada, was in truth everything I wished I could be. He was handsome, athletic, independent, and not least, readily *available*. See, I had been divorced for several years but had not been on so much as one date since my ex-husband and I called it quits. It just seemed daunting, too much of an effort. I keep to myself, well-guarded, making me the very opposite of available. When I learned that Harry was also a divorcee, I thought to myself, *why not*? Why not take a chance on this man who seemed to draw me in as if by glamour? We became close during that cruise, and soon started doing everything together, even sharing beds at night. We simply couldn't get enough. It was a sad day when the cruise ended, and he had to fly back to Canada. It took me weeks to get over it.

But we stayed in touch, much to my relief. I thought he may be the type of bachelor to soon forget the fling that we had had. But no, he answered every call, every letter, and even mailed me a few himself, always full of poetic language. We became closer and closer, even though we lived in different countries, with thousands of miles separating us. I think this was because our relationship became so rooted in language, as opposed to physical lust. We began to know each other intimately, through and through. I'd like to think we revealed ourselves fully to one another. That's why I wasn't altogether shocked when he put the question to me one late night on the phone, in the wee hours when one is most sentimental.

"You know Janice, I've been giving it a lot of thought," he said to me in his calm, measured voice. "I've told you I love you."

"I know you have. I love you too…you know that."

"Well, why are we wasting our lives apart? We both know what our hearts want. And that is certainly not to be separated. What are we waiting for?"

"What are you saying Harry?"

"Baby, why don't we just get married? We are soulmates for crying out loud!"

I feigned surprise and then asked coyly, "Harry, do you really mean it? Do you really want to marry…me?"

"Of course, I do. I wouldn't have broached the topic otherwise. Hey, I've been giving it a lot of thought. Why don't we get married on a cruise ship? I know of a couple different lines that have a special service, for a pretty penny of course. We could get married under the stars of the Bermuda Triangle. Just think!"

"Oh, Harry, I love you…"

So, it was decided. We booked the trip almost immediately and were set to sail in two weeks times. It was a whirlwind of an experience. Not only would I see the man I loved, and marry him to boot, but I would do so upon a luxury cruise liner, in my favorite hemisphere, the Western Atlantic including Bermuda and the Bahamas.

The ship we booked passage on had this so-called "North Star Observation Ball", a kind of glass enclosure ninety meters above the deck of the ship. It felt like being on the London Eye, and it commanded an impressive view of the ocean all about. Really, it was not for the faint of heart; it was very high up, and the passengers milling about on the deck below looked like ants. Harry and I quickly decided that we would hold our ceremony there. What could possibly be more memorable?

Alas, saying our vows while in Bermuda territory did not mean that our marriage was *immediately* valid. In fact, Harry told me that it could take up to six to eight weeks for our marriage certificates to arrive in the mail. But I thought *no matter, we have our entire lives in front of us*. All I was really interested in was getting married, having a wild party, and an even wilder night consummating our union. I was only slightly disturbed when Harry asked me to sign a few blank sheets of paper. He told me, very convincingly, that these would be used for future immigration purposes. See, we had planned for Harry to move immediately to my country. Everything was going to be perfect.

    The ceremony went off without a hitch, and it was everything we imagined it would be. When Harry said *I do*, I smiled and looked out over the great oceanic expanse, seeing it as a metonym for our deep love. The reception dinner was held in one of the main dining halls of the ship, and we had it catered in high style, with a multi-tiered, three-chocolate cake that dominated the center of the room, and a brass band playing wild, swinging tunes. I was drunk on love, and I basked in the envy of all our new friends we had met on the voyage, especially my contemporaries, the middle-aged woman who I considered "rivals" of sorts.

"Janice, you guys really outdid yourselves. This must have cost a fortune!"

"Yes, well, you know, my husband owns a very lucrative business."

"Janice, who did the ice sculptures? Where could you *even* get that much ice out here in the middle of Bermuda?"

"Well, Harry, he has connections. He is an international businessman."

And so, the night continued. I danced the polka with Harry, and we were the crown jewel of the floor; everyone made way for us, and I felt like a real lady. I was heady with both alcohol and excitement when we finally made our way back to the honeymooner's cabin, and the last thing I remember is Harry taking me into his arms and easing me out of my garter.

When we got back to the mainland, Harry and I had to separate for several days. I needed to prepare the house some for his arrival, and he intended to settle some business affairs before moving his "office" to my hometown. It was incredibly hard seeing him pull away in his black Jaguar, but I knew that we would be together again shortly, and this time for eternity.

I started to worry when he didn't return my calls the next day, but I chalked it up to him having a ton of important things to do in such a short timeframe. That afternoon, I received a manila envelope in the mail. It was from the authorities in Bermuda. Would we have received our marriage certificate so quickly? *Anything is possible, given my good luck of late*, I said to myself.

When I opened it, my jaw nearly fell to the floor. At first, it was more shock than heartbreak, though the latter emotion eclipsed the other in the days to follow. It was a rejection letter. The authorities informed me that they simply could not process our request, on the grounds that such a request, made on the behalf of a Mr. Harry Sanders, had been attempted too many times. I now cite the document: *Harry Sanders has requested a marriage certificate from the Hamilton City authorities 17 times. This exceeds the formal limit.*

    I never heard from Harry again, and to this day I live brokenhearted. I will never marry again.

Encounter in the South China Sea

A few years ago, we decided to take our yacht from El Nido, a beautiful beach town of Palawan island, and cross the South China Sea to Da Nang, Vietnam. Once upon a time, this used to be an exclusive route used by moderately sized sailing yachts measuring 20 feet or more. Nowadays, any average Joe with a bit of nautical know-how is bound to want to test their grit on these straits; that's why my husband and I originally thought to try it. We had been sailing for several years, but we were far from experts. In Asia this route is sometimes used for a special kind of race, notably by wealthy Japanese and Chinese living in Singapore who wish to prove their seamanship and bring prestige upon their family name. One of this race's main attractions is the opportunity to skillfully avoid one of the many Chinese military ships which patrol the waters, stationed there in order to safeguard the ports of the occupied Spratly islands. It's a game of high stakes, but success proved something beyond mere seamanship and could elevate one to the heights of a bona fide *pirate*.

We knew that the South China Sea held many pitfalls, but it was supposed to be an experience of a lifetime. We simply could not resist; and besides, we were in the prime of our lives. *Now* was the time for a grand adventure. We took three others with us, a British gentleman who was a veteran sailor with an international reputation, and two Filipino women who would handle all the menial chores aboard our yacht, such as cooking and cleaning. We started out on a very hot day. There was little to no wind, and we were forced to use the reserve engine quite a lot. We were heading east, and the sun set stealthily at our backs. We prepared to bunker down for sleep, in hopes that the morrow would bring more favorable conditions.

"There is no wind," I said to my husband. "I've never seen it so still, on any trip. I really hope our luck changes."

"Don't worry. I've read that it is sometimes this way on the South China Sea. It's enough to make one nervous, but it never lasts for more than a day or two."
I woke in the wee hours that morning and made my way onto the deck. The sky was aglow with constellations, and peace abounded, but there was still not a scrap of wind. Despite what my husband said, I was beginning to grow nervous.

That day, we discovered that we'd miscalculated our fuel levels. If no wind soon came, we'd need to turn around, or else drift aimlessly, which was not a reassuring alternative. By late afternoon of the same day, we began to experience engine problems. Our little inboard prop was overheating because we had been running it so hard. The British veteran began cursing us for being novices, and I thought at one point he was going to knock my husband clear off the deck. He had begun drinking copious amounts of rum, which made him a real handful rather than an asset.

Luckily around this time we spotted a boat in the distance. It looked to be making straight for us, thank the Lord. As it got closer, we realized it was a Chinese vessel, some sort of military speedboat which zipped across the top of the water at a considerable clip. They began making hand signs to us, but my husband and I could not discern what it was they wanted. The Brit staggered over, and though now dimwitted from booze, told us that they were using international signals which basically spelled *turn around*.

But we could not comply, though we would have gladly done so. See, our engine was overheated and there was still no wind to speak of. The Brit tried to convey this to the Chinese via a series of complicated gestures, and eventually the boat turned around and disappeared. We thought they had understood, and we all breathed a sigh of relief.

That night, while everyone aboard was fast asleep, there was an incredible crash, a ringing din that woke everyone with a start. Panicking, we rushed onto the deck. It was the Chinese vessel again, and it had rammed our yacht and thoroughly breached the hull. As the Chinese boat disappeared into the night, we realized that we were rapidly taking water. We tried to use the emergency repair kit to close the gap in the hull, but the kit was reserved for small punctures and tears. It helped very little and the yacht was in peril. All the electrical equipment became saturated, and we had no way to contact help. We could think of nothing to do but don life vests and sit on the deck. We prayed, but we all knew our time was short. The two Filipino ladies huddled in a corner and quietly wept, while my husband and I only stared over the darkening water in disbelief. The Brit was resigned to his bottle, a worthy companion for such a grim fate.

When true night fell, we saw shark fins circling the boat, as if they possessed primal intuition about the fate of our craft. Luckily, with the coming of the sun, another vessel appeared on the horizon, which did not seem to be the dreaded Chinese military ship.

As it drew alongside us, the two Filipino women started a merry, bird-like chorus, for it was a Filipino craft, namely a fishing vessel, piloted by a group of strapping young men. They swiftly took us aboard, and not too soon, for our yacht was nearly underwater. The two Filipino women embraced our saviors, and we issued our thanks, though somewhat gruffly and with an air of conceit. We thought they would take us back towards El Nido, but instead the fishermen took us to a small, unknown island, which they claimed was better "for the likes of us". The Filipino women stayed on the fishing vessel, while my husband and I, along with the Brit, got off on the little island that appeared a literal paradise.

    We were quite amazed, as there were other people on this island, a group of Japanese men who all looked ragged and exhausted, like castaways. They explained to us, while we all gathered around a fire fed by dung, that they had had a similar experience. Their vessel was also rammed by a Chinese ship of military origin, and they had managed to make it here on a lifeboat. They told us that while the island was beautiful and verdant, it was not inhabited, and there seemed to be little in the way of food or fresh water. They had quickly grown malnourished due to this fact.

Maintaining a diet only of indigenous nuts and dirty water drawn from a nearby stream, my husband and I soon became weak. Our health deteriorated by the hour; we slept fitfully through the day, and at night were both in the throes of fever dreams. I barely recall a single thing during that time, though I have this fleeting image of a wizened old Japanese man feeding us a strange concoction whose consistency was not unlike oatmeal.

One morning, we were woken by someone prodding us with their boots. Men in fancy, well-pressed uniforms stood over us. They informed us that they were Filipino customs officers, and that they had a boat which would take us back to the mainland. We found two of the Japanese "castaways" already on board, but we did not see our British veteran. Perhaps he had drunk himself to death; to this day I know nothing of his whereabouts.

An hour into the voyage back to Palawan island, one of the customs officers pulled me aside.

"Miss, do you know how long you and your husband were on that island?"

"Why, I can't say for sure, I feel like it was a lifetime…but that can't be. We were quite ill. I think we became delirious. It's hard to say."

"I wanted to ask you about the bones. We found countless skeletons, all human. It was like a great ritual had taken place; the kind of sacrifice to the gods my people made in bygone times."

I said that I couldn't tell him a thing. I knew of no bones nor sacrifices, but that I had prayed heartily to God and devil alike. I only remember that we were hungry all the time.

Nagano Gold

A good friend of mine was getting married, and what's more, he had chosen to hold the ceremony in the heart of the Nagano Basin, somewhat west of Tokyo. Naturally, I was invited. I mean, I wasn't exactly the best man or anything, but this guy and I had been buddies ever since my junior year at college. And what a wedding it turned out to be. He was never one to lack for extravagance, and his wedding was no different; he even rented a trio of Japanese clowns, *poirots* as the locals would say, who had every guest reeling with laughter, and the cake was a multi-tiered, lavish affair that was as beautiful looking as it was tasting. After the wedding concluded, my partner and I, someone who I had only recently started dating, decided to stick around for a few days and check out all the local attractions.

We took a public minibus into the wilds about Nagano, and let me tell you, there is no prettier nature to be found in the whole wide world. Surrounding you are mountains, frothing rivers, and a variety of alpine flowers which I had never seen before. It was enough to make me want to melt into the landscape, to become one with the breathtaking scenery around me. The first day of our excursion we explored the riverbeds, where boulders strewn about liberally contain fantastic minerals in a variety of colors. The air was crisp and fresh, and the river was made of snowmelt water; you could literally *smell* the ancient ice on the wind, a smell that brought me to another time and place. The best part about it, you didn't have to spend a cent up here, unlike the resort towns we were used to. Everything was free, the glorious bounty of mother nature.

The following day made an even greater impression. We trekked on over to Komake Dake, a peak located in the Central Alps that measures nearly 2600 meters. We took a bus and then a fast-moving cable car to the Komake Dake lookout, which afforded us a view over all that wild expanse. We attempted a bit of hiking and due to the great weather were able to see over the Northern Japanese Alps, an experience that will never leave me. We decided to descend by foot, which we were told would take roughly six hours if one's constitution was up to snuff. As we were making our way down, a Japanese tour guide suddenly appeared out of the blue. He was dressed strangely, in what looked like an ancient kimono, though it was considerably soiled. He told us that for a small fee he would show us a path that was both easier and more enjoyable. When I told him that we were quite content with our current route, he kept pressing us with assurances that it would be "healthier for us" to take the path that he had in mind.

Just when I was on the verge of telling him *No* for the final time, my partner saw something glittering in the nearby streambed, just where the water was pooled, making it calm and clear. We made our way over to the water's edge and started searching the sandy bed just below the surface. Suddenly, my partner screeched in excitement. He lifted his hand clear of the water and showed me its contents: a solid chunk of gold, or at least what looked like gold. It shone warmly in the alpine sun, so bright that I thought it too good to be true.

We were so overcome with excitement that we forgot about the tour guide that had just so recently badgered us about the alternative path. We hastily made our way down the mountain via the original, well-trodden path, and as soon as we reached the town, went straight to the closest exchange shop known to trade in gold.

Behind the counter was a lean Japanese man with a serious expression and cold demeanor, and when we broached the topic of selling him gold, he grew plainly suspicious, asking in broken English where we had found the gold and what the circumstances around our discovery were.

"I know you did not bring gold here on airplane. I am not stupid. ...Where you find this gold?"

"Oh, well, I...we didn't just find it. It is our gold. We were *given* this gold."

"I not believe a word. One is not given a chunk of gold. Who gave you? Or did you find this up on the mountain?"

He continued to explain that if we *had* found the gold somewhere on the mountainside, we should buy some proper equipment and continue prospecting, for we must have had natural luck concerning these things. He even ventured to say that he had equipment available, though it came with a price.

That night, in our hotel suite, we couldn't sleep a lick. We were up all night trying to decide what to do next. We were scheduled to go home the next day, but should we not stay longer? Should we try to change our travel plans, call our respective jobs, ask for more time off?

See, we thought we had stumbled upon a literal goldmine. What if there was more than just one nugget, perhaps an entire lode? We thought we could be missing out on a once in a lifetime opportunity if we did not at least go back and check it out.

We made our decision. The next morning, after paying a somewhat exuberant price to rent prospecting equipment, we tried to find the same path that had led us to the pool which we had by now begun calling *our little spot*. By late afternoon, exhausted and weary from the climb, we finally reached the selfsame spot. And like before, we immediately saw something shining just below the water's surface. In fact, the entire creek bed was aglitter, for there must have been thousands of small pieces sparkling intensely, practically offering themselves to our greedy hands. We filled our backpacks and pockets with as much as we possibly could, and so burdened made our way back to civilization. As we reached lower altitudes the lovely sounds of birdsong greeted us like heralds.

Just before nightfall we reached the village, whose margins were made up of tightly clustered ramshackle dwellings. The man who worked the exchange shop was standing in the doorway, almost as if he had been expecting us at that very moment. He smiled, and it was a smile full of knowing. Though I did not know any better at the time, I thought it contained a hint of mirth as well.

"So, my Western friends, were you so lucky again?"

My partner, beating me to it, pulled a good-sized nugget from his pocket and proudly displayed it to the shopkeeper.

"Oh yeah. You could say we were lucky again all right. More than lucky."

At this point the shopkeeper produced a small dictionary from his back pocket. He started to leaf through it, making great theatre of it all.

"My friends, there is an English word for it. If I can just find it...oh, here it is."

I looked at the dictionary, but he pulled it away from my grasp and puffed himself up as if about to deliver an important speech.

"Here it is. Fool's Gold. *Fool's* Gold. There is a Japanese saying which I think is appropriate: if you believe in something that you wish to be true, then what's called for is hard work. In your case it ended up being a little light exercise, up and down the mountain. Good for your body *and* soul!"

I looked at him sullenly, but what could we say? Had he done anything wrong? Had *we* done anything wrong? In the end he was right. We never made a cent off those damn rocks. Though our dreams of vast wealth were dashed in that instant, we still fell in love with this beautiful area and we'll be back to visit again. That is, if we ever have enough money for it.

Dining with the Captain

We all have this image of a cruise ship. What it is supposed to smell like, look like, *feel* like. Sofia was no different, and to all outward appearances, this cruiser met the stock criteria she had in mind. There were the expansive halls which seemed to lead nowhere and everywhere; the incredible indoor waterpark to rival the wonders of Disney World; the spacious dining hall where everything was covered in gilt; even a splendid prow where one could take the gratuitous selfie which seemed to pop up on every casual seafarer's Facebook feed.

Nevertheless, Sofia was feeling down this afternoon. The hour was just before twilight, when the ship turned ghostly before the diners, the myriad retirees, parents, and toddlers, came scampering down to take their places at the continental buffet. She looked out upon the sea and the declining sun and wondered why she wasn't happy, given that she was here upon this luxury cruiser, experiencing the holiday she had saved so thriftly for. The food was excellent, the entertainment satisfying, especially the standup comedy she had attended the night before which had the entire crowd doubling over in raucous laughter. She had danced with strangers in the ballroom, looking into eyes that held no mystery, but only a kind of blatant, dull lust.

Yes, she thought. *That is what I am missing. I've been lying to myself all long. I did not schedule this trip for relaxation, to sit idly poolside while children screamed more shrilly than gulls. I did not save my hard-earned salary just to fill myself up on a buffet. I came here to find love. The kind of love one sees in the movies. Real love.*

Her fellow passengers were starting to arrive for dinner. They seemed pulled from all strata of life:

businessman with trophy wives decked in pearls and diamonds; there were middle-class retirees in Hawaiian shirts, sandals, sporting their Macy's finest. Next came the younger couples struggling with packs of children, looks of strain and anxiety etched on their faces. Parrots flapped in their cages, disturbed by the magnitude of it all.

As if one, the passengers tucked into their meals after visiting the buffet counter. They ate with relish, the crystal ware ringing and flashing.

Then, a hush fell across the crowd. Many paused eating. Their gazes assumed qualities of envy, study, even some subtle alarm. It was the captain. This was made plain by his attire, the rich gold embroidery which dressed his uniform, and the smart hat which crowned his head at the perfect angle. But it was not only this that marked him, which caused the entire dining hall to pull up short. Rather, there was a certain *air* of authority about him, what Sofia would later describe as a visible aura. Where he walked, he was bathed in a yellow light, as if lit by some spotlight unbeknown to the passengers. He smiled, and Sofia felt a thrill of excitement run through her. She was certain that every other passenger felt similarly.

Slowly, everyone resumed their dinners, but where the captain went to make his greetings, entire tables would stare agape at him, as if they had lost the mechanism of speech. Nevertheless, due to his charm, he would draw the passengers out of their strange spell, and when he did so, they would chat more freely than they ever had before. Passengers found themselves speaking to this young captain as if he was their most intimate confidant. When he moved to the table where Sofia sat, her eyes followed his dream-like aura, and when he nodded his head cordially at the diners, a gold dust seemed to hang about his head like a strange halo. But she soon forgot this as he approached her. Her pulse quickened, though her mind seemed to relax.

'How do you do miss?' he asked her.

'Oh, I'm doing quite fine…I'm…this ship…'

'I'm the captain. This is my boat and my crew. My name is Jonathon. Captain Jonathon Perry. And your name?'

'Sofia….and I'm here to find love. I'm lonely captain, so terribly lonely'.

'My dear Sofia, and why is that? You can tell your captain'.

'I don't usually talk like this…you know, I didn't mean to say that just now…I meant to say...I'm having a splendid time Captain, it's great…actually, I'm lonelier than you can imagine. I've cried myself to sleep every night aboard this ship.'

The captain looked at her piercingly. She thought him the most beautiful being that ever existed. His hair, now that he had removed his hat, was the color of barely and the halo about him more intense than ever. A kind of benevolent light shone from his eyes, which danced with mirth.

'My lady, you will find love aboard this ship. Just bid your time. It will come…'.

Once the Captain had left her table Sofia found that she could not fathom what made her expose her deepest secret to him. She felt *released* by him the further he made his way from her, but she continued to follow him and his beautiful golden aura about the dining hall. She noticed that other passengers seemed compelled in a similar manner. *Strange*, Sofia thought. *You'd think we had a magician of sorts about us.* The last she saw of him that night he was leaving the dining hall, none too discreet, with a beautiful brunette wearing a fur boa. All the while the lady's husband picked idly at what was left on his plate and stared blankly out at the now moon-lit water.

The following night a grand ball was to be held, the most significant since their departure. They would anchor for several days at a port town on the morrow, and the program, which Sofia found had been slipped through her cabin's door slot as she slept, proclaimed that the crew wanted to make this night 'special and magnificent' for their guests. They would party in 'high style' and forget the cares of the world for a time.

When Sofia arrived at the scheduled hour, she found the party in full swing. Where the band on previous nights was constrained, they now played wildly. Parrots, once caged, now roamed free, perching here and there on tables and talking madly. In place of the usual staff, there were small, elderly men who vaguely resembled elves hurrying about. Even the guests seemed charged; they danced a savage rhythm, reserved women now gyrating provocatively while the men hooted. Sofia could not deny her initial alarm, but soon found herself drawn into the atmosphere, letting go of herself and inhibitions. She danced with the men she just a short time ago detested, and she *enjoyed* it. She couldn't have enough, enough *fun*. A monkey wearing a sailor's cap hung from one of the girders.

She suddenly spotted the captain. Looking no less magnificent than the previous night, he danced with the dazzling brunette he had left the dining hall with. She wore a gown out of a storybook, seemingly patched together with myriad small flowers. She glowed, and the rubies about her hair reflected the radiant golden aura of the captain. The last thing Sofia remembered was their twirling image, the captain leading her, and a look of baleful hunger in his eyes.

The next morning, the brunette was nowhere to be found. Her husband was in shambles. He couldn't remember what happened at the party. The night had been a blur. A search was conducted, but no trace of the young woman was found. The search party, with Sofia among them, finally decided to confront the captain and made their way to the ship's command center.

Instead of finding the young captain at the control board, they confront an elderly gentleman in attire identical to that of Jonathon Perry. He was incredibly disheveled and reeked of rum.

'What do you all want?' he croaked. 'A captain must get his beauty rest'.

Several passengers exclaimed together, 'Where is the young captain? Where is the beautiful girl, Miss Pennypacker?' 'Who are you!?'

The crowd gathered around the captain, who looked at them defiantly and said, suddenly in a voice gone sober, 'I knew a Miss Pennypacker long ago…she wore the Queen's gown. Yes, yes. Those were the days of my youth. The summer of my life. Now, leave an old man in peace.'

When Sofia returned to her cabin, she removed her garments and ran water for a bath. Still shaken by the disappearance of both the young captain and the young lady, she reviewed her features in the mirror. What greeted her was the visage of an old woman, prune-like, in years far past her prime. She recoiled in horror and then thought:

That advert was not kidding when it said this cruise was "one for all ages".

The Stowaway

My husband and I are a retired couple living peacefully along the southern reaches of the great state of Florida. We thought for our silver wedding that we deserved to take our seldom used sailing yacht for an extended cruise. And what better place for such a trip than the western parts of the Caribbean, where childhood dreams, full of pirates and booty, still fester? Everybody has a secret and ours is the fact that we are *hiding* something in the territory they now call the Cayman Islands. Let me just go ahead and spill the beans: we keep a lavish yacht docked in a nondescript Caribbean town, where nobody knows us and the locals duly keep to their own business.

Our yacht is a beautiful sight. We strive to keep her sparking clean, and despite her advanced age and the numerous adventures we have had on it, it continues to provide us a grand time every time we step onboard.

This is in no small part thanks to my husband's high competence behind the wheel; in fact, he is a real ace sailor! In a nutshell, she is a sailing yacht for fair weather cruising but still suited for traveling long distances.

In spite of this somewhat idyllic picture I am painting for you, my dear reader, last September everything came to a terrible head. Berry (my husband) and I decided to travel a brand-new route, from the Cayman Islands all the way to Central America, namely Honduras. I have to admit that we dared not embark on this journey alone. We decided that a friend of my husband, Dieter, should join us; another deckhand can never be a bad thing, especially when traversing the watery unknown. He lived in the Caimans and we planned for him to come aboard just before leaving port.

    Truth is, I never liked this Dieter very much. He was German and spoke English with a hard, guttural accent. We met him rarely, and he didn't seem to fit our tastes at all. My personal impression has always been that he drank too much and was financially destitute. But Berry thought a lot of him, mainly because he knew something about sailing. He was also quite the comedian, or at least Berry thought so. He also claimed to be a professional diving instructor, and of course I believed it. After all, the Cayman Islands are still a diver's paradise. Anyway, we took him with us because he had been pestering my husband for the longest time to cross to Honduras. He said that urgent business was waiting for him there, and as it turned out, that was true to a certain degree.

After some preparation, we were on our way, and the significantly advanced technology of our yacht allowed us to sail without much effort and navigate spritely westwards with a tailwind. The closer we came to the Central American coast, the more exuberant we felt. At least my husband and I did. However, our

German guest became more and more fretful, asking almost hourly about the remaining travel time.

"The weather is getting worse the further west we get," Berry said in a worried voice. Although the sea was calm, the horizon actually appeared unusually grey, like a dark bruise swelling in the distance.

"Our ship will weather a storm, right darling?"

"A ship can usually take more punishment than its passengers," answered Berry, grinning like a fool.

"What about that German? Dieter just sits in the corner and broods."

"I don't know. Something seems to be bothering him."

"Maybe you should talk to him."

"Honey, there's no need. Let's leave him be. I'm sure he has his reasons. Besides, he needs to stay focused on navigating."

"I think I see land yonder," I cried.

"We'll be moored in Roatan in an hour. Don't worry babe."

"Why does that plastic wrapping move so curiously? There, up at the bow."

Berry grunted. He slowly approached the animated plastic and ripped it aside. A piercing scream followed. We couldn't believe it. A frail, bedraggled woman was kneeling where the sheet had been. She appeared out of her wits, looking about with wild eyes.

"Who are you and how the hell did you get on my ship?"

The woman muttered something in Spanish.

"What is she saying, Berry? What is she doing here?"

Berry understood a few words. "The woman seems to be begging for something. She says she boarded in the Caymans. I think she wants to go… home."

"Where is that?"

"Honduras. Apparently."

"What kind of crazy coincidence is this? Berry, do something!"

"Hey Dieter, did you see this woman get on board?"

He just shook his head and looked out on the water forlornly.

Even though Dieter sat in silence, I could see in his eyes that he recognized this stowaway.

"Let's just help the woman," I said dejectedly. What choice do we have?

Suddenly, strong gales buffeted our craft and rain came down in dazzling sheets. An hour later we were fortunate enough to reach the harbor at Rohan. We had hardly docked when the storm broke out with redoubled might. The wooden pier seemed to sway beneath us.

We moored our boat and immediately went to the harbor pub, which doubled as a kind of hotel. In this weather we really didn't feel like looking further for room and board.

We were hardly in our rooms when there was a knock at the door. An unknown young man tried to explain in broken English that our friend, Dieter, was in some kind of trouble in the house just next door. Berry was pulling a poncho over his head when the man insisted that we both needed to go. What a crazy it had turned into!

He led us to the small, unremarkable house. "Your friend is upstairs," he said. But no sooner had we stepped inside than he closed the door behind us. We heard the lock driven home. We were trapped! Now I was panicking and Berry was verging on violence. With a warrior's bellow, he splintered the door with his bare fists. We rushed outside and the wind gusted about us. It was now fully night. I pointed to the pier.

"The boat! Where did she go?"

It was nowhere to be seen. We ran up and down the pier like mad people, the rain soaking us to the bone.

"Could it be that the storm tore her away?"

"No way. This was a setup! Dieter!"

It was past midnight when the police finally arrived at our "hotel". God knows why it took them so long. Nothing we said seemed to matter, and the paperwork we filled out appeared a mere formality. We carried nothing but a few dollars, and our passports had been on the yacht. There was no sign of Dieter and the mysterious woman.

Two days later, we arrived exhausted and depressed at the airport in Tegucigalpa, equipped with temporary passports from the American embassy. We were waiting in line for the security check when someone tentatively tapped me on the shoulder. It was the stowaway! She proceeded to cry and cry. It turned out that she could speak a few words of English; at least, enough for us to get the gist of it. She was so sorry for everything that had befallen us. Berry and I were just stunned. She admitted everything. She claimed it had been Dieter's idea to steal from us. He had meticulously planned it all, down to the theft of our treasured yacht. She ended by saying she had only complied because she loved the man.

She then handed us a plastic bag. I looked inside and couldn't believe it: our passports and my empty wallet!

"There's more in the bag," she said. Surprisingly, I discovered a tattered German passport. We recognized his smug face immediately. Only his name was different: Willi Mayer.

Once back home we went through the seven circles of Hell to bring the bastard down. May God have mercy on his lying soul.

Strangers on an Ocean Liner

This was the fifth couple to have been murdered on a cruise ship this way. Elizabeth had been tracking the cases, realizing with growing horror that, yes, whoever was doing this was targeting specific people. Young newlyweds, most of them artists or artistically inclined. The man had blond hair and his eyes were closed, he was sun-kissed from tanning on the cruise. His wife, a slim and beautiful redhead that reminded Elizabeth of her own daughter. This woman, like Julia, had been pale and had a dancer's body, barely visible when the wind blew her long swimsuit cover close to her frozen body.

    She didn't think the police had made connections yet. After all, technically these murders were being done in open water, with no centralized judicial system meant to investigate.

    This one was on a pleasure cruise around the Caribbean. They had been posed on the top deck, in the middle of the night, their faces sewn together as though they were trying to become one, their fingers entwined and branded so that the flesh was melted in place. Kneeling, facing each other. Their mouths had been stitched up at the corners into matching loving smiles.

Elizabeth felt sick to her stomach, biting her lower lip and restlessly petting her red hair, streaked with gray, watching the police cordon off the area when they landed in Jamaica. She was within a crowd of guests, all of them whispering to each other with low, horrified voices. A lot of people were couples on this cruise – she was one of the older guests, and notably single compared to the rest of them.

She swallowed, and approached one of the officers guarding the line. He was a large dark-skinned man, with a balding head sweating in the sun and a grim expression on his round face. He held his hand up to her to stop her getting closer.

"Ma'am, please step back," he said sternly.

"Is the woman burned?" she asked. He frowned at her. "On her lower back. Check if she's been burned." The man's frown deepened, but he turned, waving over one of the investigators near the bodies. They exchanged quick words to each other, and the investigator frowned at Elizabeth. "What's your name?" he asked.

"Elizabeth Monroe," she replied.

"Inspector Gray," he said, and shook her hand. He was smaller than his companion, but had the same dark complexion, sweating in his brown uniform. He had one blue eye, the other brown, and she found herself looking between the mismatched irises, searching for answers.

"What's this about a brand?"

"My -." Elizabeth swallowed, choking back emotion. "My daughter was killed on a cruise ship. She had been on her honeymoon, and this is -. This is the fifth set I've known about, that I've read about.

My daughter was branded, and I know at least two of the other couples were as well. You need to check, to see if it's the same people."
She was certain that it was, but knowing that would confirm it.
Gray eyed her for a moment more, and then nodded to his colleague. "Let her through," he said. She bowed under the police tape and walked with him towards the bodies, swallowing down her emotions as she saw the couple entwined in death.

Gray lifted the back of the woman's shirt, and Elizabeth clutched her throat, her eyes welling with tears when she saw that the woman had been branded, just like her daughter. Her sweet, precious Julia.

The woman had a cross burned into the small of her back. Elizabeth had the strangest urge to touch it, to feel the crisped edges of the skin. She resisted. She had done the same to Julia, when she'd been called in to claim and identify her body. She could still remember how the raised skin had felt, black and cold beneath her touch.

She closed her eyes, and a single tear fell. "They did it again," she whispered.

Gray made a sound, and then yelled loudly; "Lock down the ship! No one comes on or off."

"They won't be here anymore," Elizabeth warned. "They never are."

"Ms. Monroe, please step back and let me do my job."

Elizabeth was herded back into place behind the tape with the other rubberneckers. She swallowed, righteous anger and nausea welling up in her stomach. No, she couldn't let whoever had done this get away with it a fifth time.

There had been no tours scheduled – this wasn't meant to be a day where the ship stopped. The bodies had been discovered early in the morning, before most of the other guests were awake. Surely, she thought, surely whoever had done this would still be on board.

She had been following the various cases religiously. Everyone had an alibi on the ships where people had been murdered – of course they did. But someone must have stood out.

She thought about the demographics on this particular cruise. She assumed it had to be a couple, because that would be the easiest way to blend in, and one party could vouch for the other when it came to alibis. They would have to be young, and strong enough to subdue other young, strong people.
So no one elderly.

They would have to be approachable, so that their victims didn't feel afraid around them, so that they could lure their prey close enough to kill. Be able to blend in. So, white, she assumed, because most of the people on this cruise ship were white. A man and a woman, since a gay couple would stand out more.

Her eyes searched the deck of the ship. The group of onlookers was getting larger now, as word began to spread. Most of them were staring, wide-eyed, at the scene in front of them. She could understand that; the first few instances had horrified her, and the police reports, the journalist papers, none of them had held back in terms of detail.

"It's horrible, isn't it?"

Elizabeth's attention was drawn at the question. Beside her stood a woman, in her late twenties. Her hair was long and black, her eyes the same bright blue as the cloudless sky above them. She was slim and gorgeous, exactly the kind of woman you would expect to see on a cruise ship. Beside her stood a man, with the same dark hair and bright eyes. He was skinny as well, but muscled, his tanned skin hinting at powerful strength in his shoulders and arms.

She cleared her throat when the woman's eyes turned to her. "It is," she replied with a nod.
The woman smiled. "You look like you could use a drink," she said kindly. She gestured to the man beside her. "Alex and I have some stuff stored away in our cabin. Would you like to join us?"

Elizabeth frowned. What kind of people would smile and drink on a morning like this? "No, thank you," she replied. "I think I'll stay…?"

This girl looked pathetic, Elizabeth thought. There was no engagement or wedding ring on her hand, and this odd couple looked similar enough that Elizabeth would have assumed they were related, had they not been on a couple's cruise.

Their hands met, fingers lacing. "Is this your first time on a cruise?" the young woman asked.

"Yes," Elizabeth said. "Yours?"

"Oh, no," she said with a playful giggle. Her bubbly demeanor was unnerving. "Mz real name is Margaret and my partner Alex and I are old hats at this." She looked up at the man, an adoring smile on her face. "This is our fifth one this year, and I think we're going to have a lot more before we're through."

Elizabeth frowned, and cleared her throat. She saw Gray approaching the yellow tape. "Well, I hope the rest are less eventful than this one."

Margaret laughed, in a way that sent a shiver down Elizabeth's spine. She couldn't help but look at the couple again. They looked *so* similar to each other; they could have been brother and sister. Margaret fiddled with a necklace around her neck. It was a silver chain, and hanging from it was a large cross.

A dark curl of suspicion started in her chest.

"So, what cabin number are you in?" Elizabeth asked. "I might take you up on that offer later."

"30-A," Alex said, speaking for the first time. They had the same accent. Texan, or from one of the Carolinas.

Elizabeth nodded, and hurried away, waylaying Gray as he approached the ship Captain. "Detective," she said lowly, "Captain."

"Ms. Monroe," Gray greeted with a nod.

"Do either of you have access to the ship manifesto?" Elizabeth asked. They frowned at her. She looked over her shoulder, and couldn't see Margaret or Alex in the crowd. "Who are the people in 30-A?"

The captain frowned at her, and held up a clipboard, turning the first few pages. "Alex and Margaret Cranston," he reported.

Elizabeth frowned. "Married?"

"Impossible to say," the Captain replied. "They have a single bed room, though."

"Margaret told me that they've been on multiple cruises this year," Elizabeth told Gray. "And she had a cross around her neck. I couldn't tell for certain, but it looks about the same size and shape as the one in your victim."

Gray blinked at her, surprised. "Well," he said. "I suppose I should ask Mr. and Mrs. Cranston some questions. Where are they?"

"They left," Elizabeth said, looking over her shoulder again. "They might be trying to leave the ship." Gray nodded, ducking under the tape and hurrying past her. There were stairs leading to the lower levels, and the level below had access to the outside of the ship where passengers could get on and off.

Elizabeth grabbed his arm and pointed, when she saw the familiar pair of dark-haired people. "There!" she said.

"Alex and Margaret Cranston!" Gray called. They stopped, and turned to him as he approached. He nodded to their bags. "No one is coming on or off the ship, I'm afraid. I'd like to ask you a couple of questions."

Margaret's eyes narrowed, and she looked at Elizabeth. "What's this about?" she demanded.

"There's been a murder on the ship, Mrs. Cranston. Surely you can understand we might have a few questions for some of the passengers."

"We didn't do it," Alex snapped. He held his wife's hand tightly and pulled her close to him. "My sister and I were in our cabin all night. You can ask our neighbors – they saw us go in."

"Sister," Elizabeth echoed, brows rising. "In a single bed?"

Alex winced.

Margaret glared at both of them. "That's none of your business," she said archly. "And you don't have any evidence against us that we were involved in whatever happened to those *animals*." Elizabeth blinked at her. "Flaunting themselves around like they're King and Queen of the world. Making a nuisance of themselves. You can ask anyone – they were loud and obnoxious and -." She stopped, swallowing harshly, her cheeks turning pink with outrage. "They got what was coming to them."

Gray pressed his lips together, and sighed. "I'd like you to come with me, please," he said, and gestured for a crew member to approach and assist him in the arrest. "Ms. Monroe, thank you for your assistance in this matter."

Elizabeth nodded, stepping away. Margaret narrowed her eyes at Elizabeth, free hand toying with the cross around her neck.

"Did you burn that into Julia, too?" she demanded. "My little girl. Did you kill her too?"

Margaret blinked, and then laughed cruelly. "I thought I recognized you. Looks like I saved her the trouble of getting old."

"This way, please," Gray said.

Alex wrapped his arm around Margaret, directing her to follow Gray. Elizabeth watched them go, wondering how on Earth two young, gorgeous people could have been twisted around each other so viciously. If they sought the open seas because they didn't have to hide who they were, but still couldn't bring themselves to tolerate the open affection shared by people in a legal marriage. Perhaps she would never find out, or this would be another report in a newspaper with more questions raised than answers.

Jealousy, she supposed, was as much a killer as a knife or a gun.

"I hope you rot in Hell," Margaret missed over her shoulder, as Gray took her arm and led her away.

Elizabeth pressed her lips together, and sighed, thinking that, despite having caught Julia's killer, the satisfaction of doing so wasn't going to bring her back. "I'm already there," she replied. Margaret said nothing to that, just huffed, tossed her hair, and let her and her brother be led away.

She Jumped on Her Own

It was nine o'clock on a Tuesday evening when a detective and a cop met for a drink. The night was still warm and heavy, but there was a definite breeze building in the air. They sat outside, covered by the darkness except for the dim light emanating from the small lamp set on their table. Beyond them was the Atlantic Ocean, extending out as far as the eye could see, and on a night like that, it was hard to make out anything further away than the person sitting opposite. The pair were secluded, separated from the rest of the bar by a small wall so that they in near-total privacy.

"What will you have?" The detective asked.

"I'll have a glass of white, large." The cop answered.

They spoke in low voices, even though the sound of the sea and the hum of the engine made it nearly impossible to hear much more than the faint sound of reggae music that was coming from the decks. As they ordered, the breeze picked up, so that the pair were distracted with the smells of the ocean, the fresh, salty air filling their lungs. After a few moments of hushed conversation, the drinks arrived, wine for the cop, rum for the detective. The waiter placed each drink on a single square napkin. The cop noticed him clamping down her wine quickly, so the napkin wouldn't blow away, its edges flapping helplessly in the wind.

The detective picked up his rum, as though gesturing to cheers. The cop reciprocated, picking up her wine so that their glasses came together with a *clink* in the air. As their drinks met, so did their eyes, and they both smiled.

"Happy anniversary."

The retired cop looked into her husband's deep, brown eyes, at his tanned face and at his greying hair, and smiled.

"Happy anniversary, darling."

"You look lovely tonight", Bill said, looking at Jane in her pale green dress, which so complimented her dark features.

"Thank you, dear."

"I can't believe we're finally here. We've dreamed about this for so long", Bill said.

"I know!" Jane exclaimed. "It seems like just yesterday we were working those long hours on all those crazy cases and now look at us…cruising around the islands of the Caribbean! We couldn't have asked for a better retirement."

"I agree", said Bill. "Work was great, but I'm so happy to be finally done with that chapter and to be here together. It feels so good to say that we are officially done solving cases."

"Cheers to that!"

The couple sat talking over their drinks for another hour or so, happily reminiscing about their life together. They were currently cruising around the Bahamas and had spent the entire day in Nassau exploring the port, paddling in the crystal-clear waters, and lounging on the stunning white beach. It had been an extraordinary day and one they'd never forget; they had had lunch in the town and then cocktails and fresh fruit on the beach, all the while surrounded by palm trees and stunning flowers. They had only set sail a few hours earlier and were heading down south towards Puerto Rico.

The waiter soon came round to take their order and the couple decided to stay for another drink, relishing their forty years milestone. As the new round of drinks arrived, Jane was distracted by something over Bill's shoulder.

"Look who it is", she said.

Bill turned around to where Jane was gesturing. She was looking at a man and woman around their age that had just walked into the bar area. The man was wearing a garish Hawaiian shirt and speaking very loudly, whilst the woman stood a little behind him, so that her face was partly obscured from Bill's vision. She looked a little out of place next to her husband in her muted grey dress and quiet, sensible shoes. The couple spotted Bill and Jane almost instantly and came over to them.

"Well hello there! Fancy seeing you guys here", the man said. "How's your evening going? Oh! And happy anniversary!"

The man shook Bill's hand, vigorously.

"Thank you", Jane said, as the man made a show of kissing her hand. "It's been wonderful; it's a lovely night."

"It is indeed!" The man said. "Romance is definitely in the air…"

As he spoke, he pulled his wife closer to him. He was grinning from ear-to-ear, but she seemed more reserved, only producing a small smile. Bill noticed that her nose seemed to crinkle slightly when her husband had put his arm around her. He wasn't surprised, after what they'd heard the night before.

"What's your plan for this evening then?" Bill asked.

"Ah, you know, just a few drinks with the beloved", the man replied. "Are you guys staying out for long? Fancy joining for one round?"

"Yes, that would be -"

"I'm sure they don't want us crashing their romantic evening, Harry", the woman said. "We should really let you both get back to your celebration. Don't let Harry here distract you."

She said this with a little laugh, but Jane saw that the smile didn't quite reach her eyes.

"Yes, you're right, Mary. Come on, let's leave them to it dear, we have our own evening to get to."

Jane and Bill watched as the couple walked away, Harry's arm still around Mary. They headed to a table across the decks from them and sat down, Harry pulling out Mary's chair for her. The waiter went over to their table and they were blocked from view.

"Well they seem to have sorted things out, I guess", Bill said.

"Yeah, things seem to be better…" Jane said.

But there was a note of uncertainty in both of their voices, and when they looked at each other they knew neither one of them really believed what they'd said. But they had agreed to leave work at work and stop being so skeptical. Besides, it didn't really have anything to do with them; they were just the couple staying in the cabin next to them. They had met on the first day of cruise almost two weeks before and had become quite friendly. They'd enjoyed walks along the decks together, some drinks, and even a couple of dinners, but nothing much more than that. Both Bill and Jane had genuinely enjoyed their company and felt that they got on well. The only thing that held them back was what they sometimes heard at night, through the thin walls of their cabin, at a time when the couple clearly thought no one would be listening. As Jane looked at Bill, she could tell they were both thinking about those occasions, when all they could hear was the distinct sound of shouting, and sometimes screaming, coming from that couple in Cabin 201.

It was nearly eleven when Jane suggested they call it a night and head back to their cabin. Bill agreed, so they settled the tab and headed out of the bar area. There was no sign of Harry and Mary.

"They must've gone back to their cabin already", Bill said, knowing that Jane had noticed their absence too.

This was one of best things about living with a cop, Bill thought, is that he never had to over-explain or worry that he wouldn't be understood, because Jane noticed everything that he did, and sometimes more.

"Well Mary didn't exactly look up for it, did she?" Jane said.

"No", Bill agreed, "she definitely didn't."

They put their curiosity about the couple next door out of their minds, however, as they walked along the decking in the direction of the cabins. Instead they spoke about their evening, giving each other more affirmations of their love and feelings of content and security. When they reached their cabin, they noticed that the one next door, Cabin 201, was empty. It was clear that Harry and Mary, wherever they were, were not in their room. The husband and wife exchanged glances but said nothing as they unlocked their door and got ready to go to bed.

It was several hours later when the couple were woken by a noise coming from outside their cabin.

"Not again", Bill groaned. "Why do they have to choose the middle of the night to have their shouting matches?"

"Wait, Bill", Jane said, quietly. "I don't think it's coming from their room. And I don't hear a woman's voice. Listen."

They were quiet for a moment, both listening to the commotion going on outside. Bill quickly realized that his wife was right - the shouting seemed to be coming from the corridor, not from the room next door, and while he was pretty sure he could hear Harry's voice, he definitely couldn't hear Mary's, but rather the voice of one or perhaps two other men.

"What time is it?" Bill asked, searching for his phone.

"About half past four", Jane said. "What do you think's going on out there? I could swear one of the men speaking is the porter who helped us to our room."

"I think you might be right", Bill said. "So what on earth could they be going on about this morning?"

"Bill, do you think one of us should pop out and see what's going on? They might not realize that we can hear them and…I don't know…I feel like something's happened."
Bill looked at his wife and had a hunch at what she was getting at.

"Ok", he said. "I'll go."

Jane watched as her husband put on his dressing gown and headed out of the room. When he opened the door, the shouting got louder, but he didn't close it fully behind him. Jane suspected he had left it open for her so she could hear. She listened carefully as Bill showed himself to the group, and she could hear him speaking.

"I'm sorry to interrupt but is everything okay out here? I'm not sure if you know but the walls aren't the thickest and we couldn't help overhearing…"

But Bill had been interrupted, and from the sounds of it was Harry who was speaking.

"Bill, something awful has happened!"
But Jane couldn't make out the rest of what Harry was saying because he had started crying. She thought she could hear one of the other men speaking, in very low tones, perhaps made aware how much their voices were

carrying. It carried on like that for another couple of minutes until Jane heard Bill speaking again.

"I see", he said. "Let me go and fetch my wife and we'll meet you in the restaurant."

Before Bill had even closed the door behind fully, Jane had got out of bed and was putting on her own dressing gown.

"What's happened?" She whispered.

"It's Mary…she's dead."

"What?" Jane said, completely stunned.

"According to the porter, she and Harry were walking along the decking and she fell over the rails. I couldn't get much out of Harry as I'm sure you heard but the coast guard have been informed. Anyway, they need us to help them with Harry's statement and so on, and I think it's better we hear it together."

Jane put her slippers on, still in shock, and followed Bill out into the corridor back towards the restaurant.

She sat at the table in the middle were Harry and two male members of staff. Harry was no longer crying but he looked terrible. The other two men weren't saying anything, but rather were sat there looking solum, and slightly awkward. They seemed almost relieved when they spotted Bill and Jane coming towards them. Once they had taken their seats, Jane spoke.

"Harry, I'm so sorry", she said.

Harry looked up at her and smiled weakly.

"Thank you, Jane."

"Harry", Bill said in a kind voice, "do you think you could take us through what happened tonight?"

"Where shall I start from?" Harry asked.

"Wherever you think is important", Jane said, gently. "What about when you saw us earlier in the bar?"

"Verz well", Harry began, his voice shaking a little. "So, we…err…we saw you at the bar."

"And what time would you say that was?" Bill asked.

"Gosh, I don't know. Maybe around ten? Does that matter? I honestly can't remember."

"That's ok", Bill said. "That sounds right. Please, carry on."

"Right", Harry said. "So yeah, we saw you at around ten o'clock. Then we got a drink, Mary and I, but we didn't stay in the bar for long - only about an hour or so, because you guys were still there when we left. We decided to go and check out the bar on the other side of the ship because we heard there was live music there going on. It took us a while to get there - Mary was a little unsteady on her feet but she'd always been nervous on boats, see. Anyway, we reached the other bar and had a couple more drinks each. There wasn't any music, but it was pleasant all the same."

"Do you remember who served you there?" Jane asked. "Can someone confirm when you were there?"

"Why?" Harry asked, a little defensively.

"It's just helpful for us to have", Jane said.

Her voice was still calm, but the gentle tone had subsided slightly.

"At what time did you leave the bar?" Bill asked.

"I honestly don't know", Harry said. "We were there for a couple of hours, at least, maybe more. Actually, I think it was nearing two o'clock when we decided to make a move."

"And then what did you do?"

"Well Mary said she wasn't feeling well so we decided to go back to our cabin but - well she thought that a walk would make her feel better so we decided to walk for a bit before and then we walking by the railings and then Mary was swaying so much and before I knew it…before I realized what was happening…Mary was dead."

But Harry was crying again. It seemed to render him speechless.

"Why don't we get some tea and coffee? And perhaps some toast or something", Jane said.

"Good idea", said one of the porters.

Around ten minutes later, the porter came back to the restaurant with two pots of tea and coffee and an assortment of toast and croissants. It was nearly half-past five in the morning and the sky was brightening. Jane could feel it was already getting warmer and as the porter was laying out the food, her eyes drew to the sea where she could tell a beautiful sunrise was about to unfold.

"Why don't you accompany Harry to get some food?" Bill said to the remaining porter.

He obliged without comment. Harry got up slowly and followed him silently. As soon as they were out of earshot Bill turned to Jane.

"Did you notice?" He said, quietly.

"Yes", she said. "No tears…"

"Exactly", said Bill. "And his story…"

"I know."

But before they could say anymore the three men were making their way back towards the table, bringing with them coffees for Bill and Jane.

"Right", Bill began again. "Harry, I know this is hard, but we need you to please take us through, in more detail, what exactly happened when you went walking."

"I told you", Harry said. "We went walking, and we were walking along the rails because Mary wanted to see the sea and she wanted to have something to hold on to. She was very unsteady, like I said she's not a fan of boats, and then - I was looking the other way - I saw out the corner of my eye that she seemed to be leaning too much on the rails. And then suddenly she was gone."

"She fell over the rails?" Bill asked.

"Of course she fell over the rails", Harry said. "She didn't just vanish into mid-air, did she?"

"Well you tell me", Bill said.

"Look, what's going on here?" Harry said, puffing out his chest slightly. "My wife is dead! And all you can do is ask these stupid questions!"

"See, this is where I'm confused", Bill said, calmly. "You keep saying your wife is dead. Now I know it is very unlikely given the current of the ocean, not to mention the temperature, but Mary is at this time a missing person. The coast guard is searching for her as we speak. We have every possible person on this case looking for her, but you seem so sure that she is dead."

"What on earth! Of course she's dead! Don't try and tell me otherwise…don't try and raise my hopes…don't you dare…"

"No one is trying to give you false information, Harry", Jane said. "What we are after are the facts, and that will only help you, and Mary."

Bill nodded in agreement.

"Tell me something, Harry", Bill said. "You say your wife doesn't much care for boats, that they make her nervous."

"Yes, they made her very unsteady", Harry said.

"So why did you come on a cruise?" Bill said.

"W-what?!" Harry said, looking completely flustered. "What do you mean? We went for the same reason you did probably! We went to spend time together!"

"It just seems to me", Bill said, his voice still measured, "that if my wife didn't like boats, we wouldn't go on a cruise."

"But Mary *wanted* to go! She was just…Mary was just a nervous person!"

"And why," Bill said, interrupting Harry, "do you keep referring to your wife in the past tense when we've told you that she is a missing person at this time."

"I - I…what does it even matter!"

Harry was beside himself; he could barely speak. He had stood up and was staring around for who knew what, still trying to get the words out. Bill, Jane and the two porters all sat still, watching him.

Then the phone rang. Everyone stared at the porter as he stood up to go and answer it.

"Hello", he said.

There was a minute of silence where no one moved.

"I see", they heard the porter say. "I'll let them know now."

He put the phone down and sat back down at the table.

"That was the coastguard. They've found Mary. She's dead."

No one said anything, waiting for the porter to finish.

"And there's something else. They haven't done a formal review yet, but they say she didn't drown. They say she died from blunt force trauma to the head."

They all turned to Harry, and there was fear in his eyes.

"I think it's time you start telling the truth, Harry", Bill said.

"Do you really want to know?" Harry said, his tone suddenly changing. "It's a hell of a story…"

Escape from Venice

"Here we are, madam."

The waiter handed me the bill. It seemed normal at first; the final number was steep but that was standard for the Rudder Club. We'd come for lunch for my husband, Mike's, fortieth birthday with our friends Sophie and Henry, who were another couple. As it was a celebration, I had suggested we come to the Club, as my husband and I were members (we'd all agreed to spend a little extra when we all turned forty). So, I hadn't thought anything of the price at first, and it had taken me a few moments to realize there was something wrong.

"Excuse me, sorry but I think we've been overcharged. Ah, yes see here - we didn't order this bottle. And we only ordered one plate of the grilled salmon."

"Are you sure?"

"I'm quite sure, unless someone's slipped a whole salmon into their bag without anyone noticing."

Everyone around the table laughed.

I passed the bill to Mike so he could double-check. I watched him study the bill, his sandy hair falling into his light eyes. We were the antithesis of each other, him with pale features and light complexion, me with brown hair and tanned skin. He was wearing a grey suit, one I had bought him especially, and I couldn't help but admire him in that moment as he concentrated so seriously on the receipt. I looked at his green pocket square, which I had bought him, I had to admit, because it matched my green dress.

"You're right, Charlotte", Mike said, handing the bill back to the waiter.

"I see. Let me go and investigate that now."

The waiter hurried off back to the front of the restaurant, still looking slightly skeptical.

"Well, he was rather rude, is he new?" Sophie asked.

"Oh, he was nothing. We've had much worse situations, believe me" I said with a little smile, "if only this man knew how I'd handled that situation…"

"Oh", Sophie responded, intrigued. "Do tell."

"Yes, come on Charlotte, you always have the best stories", Henry said from across the table.

"Ok, ok…" I said, with a little laugh. "It was when we were on our honeymoon, you know when Mike and I took that cruise…"

I gazed out of the window, letting the sight of the boats in the harbour take me back to that time, those wonderful months spent in wedded bliss, and I began to tell the story.

We'd been on the cruise for about a month or so; the ship was huge, one of those cruises with a swimming pool, a dozen bars and restaurants. We'd spent the last month travelling all around Italy. The weather had been beautiful, and we had spent many a day sunbathing on the decks of the ship, and swimming in the sea.

It was late September when we reached the port of Venice. When we stepped off the boat, we were overwhelmed with what we saw, stunning waters and a sea of terracotta and white buildings. The only downside was the weather. We didn't think to take an umbrella with us so of course it was pouring with rain the entire time, the kind of biblical rain that pavement off the streets and has you drenched in seconds. The streets were flooded; it was something we'd never seen before

"That sounds quite romantic", Sophie interjected.

I laughed.

"We thought so too, at first."

We felt like we were in a film; we were ready to embrace the dramatic romance of the rain. Venice felt like ours because there was barely anybody there. We held hands and ran down the narrow streets feeling like a couple of teenagers. We admired the colourful architecture and the quaint balconies aligned with plants. We took in the numerous little bridges and the cobbled ground, the parts that were still visible through the water shining. Of course, after a while the novelty wore off and we both caught sight of each other. A pair of drowned rats, feet sodden, the water up to our ankles. Our legs were splattered with mud and covered in goosebumps. The market stalls and outdoor cafes had closed because of the rain so we had to take refuge in a little coffee shop that we'd found.

  Then we learned that the flood meant we couldn't get back to the ship that night. Apparently, the usual smaller boats that took us from the cruise to the towns weren't willing to run. So we were stuck in the rain, in the *flood*, for the whole night.

"Goodness! Wouldn't anyone take you?" Henry said.

"Well we tried to bribe someone to take us", I said. "You know, one of those small boats or gondolas or something…but you see it's quite difficult to bribe someone when your husband has left all of your cash on the cruise…"

The others laughed and Mike did a mocking look of shame.

I continued with the story, explaining how our only option was to find somewhere to stay - and it had to be cheap because we only had a very small amount of cash on us (enough for a cheap meal but definitely not enough to bribe someone out there). There were lots of restaurants with rooms to rent as we walked down the street, but they all seemed too expensive.

Then one place caught our eye - they'd all shoved their menus at us as we walked down but their prices actually seemed ok. They said it was about twenty-five euros for a fillet of fish, decent, so we stopped there, deciding that was probably our best bet, and it looked authentic. It looked perfectly nice as well. We asked about their rooms and if they had availability and they said yes, they did and that someone would reserve us a room and would come down to discuss the price with us while we ate. Again, the rooms seemed to be at a decent rate so we thought it looked like a good place to stay for the night until we could get back to the cruise ship.

We sat outside on a little table; it was relatively empty, but the rain had at least stopped. As we ordered our food, I noticed that the waiter did not look Italian and as I looked around it occurred to me that no one working there seemed to be, and I couldn't hear anyone speaking Italian. We realised that the staff were Middle Eastern and were in fact speaking what we thought was Arabic.

The food arrived reasonably quickly but it was over-cooked - just edible but just not what we were hoping for. We had been sold a traditional Italian meal but instead it seemed we'd hit upon a tourist restaurant run by a Middle Eastern family that had no idea how to cook an Italian dish at all. After dinner, one of the other waiter's showed us to our room, giving us a quote for the price and everything. The room, as I had kind of expected by this point, was nothing special. It was dingy and a very strange smell. As we walked through the building, we quickly replied the rest of the hotel was the same; it looked like it had been neglected for several years; the carpets were heavily stained and the walls were peeling. And the smell - it seemed to linger everywhere. Plus no one seemed to be working there; there was no one at reception for ages.

We checked out early, ready to head back to the cruise as quickly as possible. We sat down as we waited for our bill, looking at all the other people out for breakfast filling up the streets.

"So the bill finally arrives and you'll never believe what they tried to charge us… 600 euros!" I said. "It was extortionate!"

"No!" Henry and Sophie exclaimed together.

"I know! 600 euros for a smelly room and some overcooked fish!"

Obviously, we were completely outraged thinking they were taking advantage of us. We disputed the bill, but the waiter kept insisting that everything was correct and that the room and our meal were worth 600 euros. It didn't take long for the situation to turn nasty. The owner got involved and within about thirty seconds it seemed like his whole family and their partners had joined in too so that we were outnumbered, and they were all shouting. They'd clearly increased their numbers to try and intimidate us. We were completely surrounded. Everyone on the street was looking at us by then - it must have looked like a sight - an obviously foreign couple sat on some tiny table surrounded by about twenty-odd people all aggressively yelling at them in Arabic. A couple of police officers walked past at one point and I honestly thought that the owner had rung the police on us! We were outnumbered by a very large and very angry Middle Eastern family. The police officers didn't get involved though - I think they were just keeping their heads down and praying no one brought them into to be honest.

We couldn't see how on earth we were getting out of this. They were clearly trying to scam us but I we were completely outnumbered. And then to make things worse…we could hear the horn in the distance warning people that the ship was leaving. We tried to explain to the family that that was our cruise ship - we pointed it out to them - telling them that the cruise would leave if we didn't get back to the ship in the next ten minutes. But they wouldn't let us leave! The owner said we were robbing them. He kept insisting that he'd told us the prices upfront and that the fish was priced by the gram and that this had all been very clear. He was shouting at me, his face very close to mine, so close that I had felt drops of his spit on my face. At this Mike stood up, obviously furious.

"It was disgusting!" Mike interjected. "They were absolutely foul."

I explained how then the horn sounded again, another warning, but the family were swarming in on us.

A couple of the men had a hold of Mike and were threatening him. I was getting so stressed - all I cared about was getting back to that ship before it left us stranded here in Venice with no money and a mob on our backs.

'Look, we need to be back on that ship in less than ten minutes!' I had said. 'We have no cash on us and the only way you'll get your money is if we go back to that ship!'

'Fine', said the owner, 'one of our guys will take you back to the ship, but you must pay him the money in cash once you reach the ship. Otherwise he will bring you back here and we will call the police on you.'

I can't express how annoyed we were, seeing things were getting desperate - there were just so many of them and it felt like they were on top of us! I couldn't see anything beyond the clan of people that had us trapped. I told them we would agree to give the guy the money only if he took us to the ship right away. We finally seemed to come to an agreement and the owner got one of his brothers to organise a small boat to take us there. To add even more stress to the situation the boat didn't even have an engine - just rudders! We were tight for time as it was so this was just getting ridiculous. We hurried onto the boat and the man set sail towards to cruise ship, bringing two of his brothers with him (presumably to keep us outnumbered and make sure we didn't do a runner with the money - I mean where were we going to run to; we were going to a ship!).

The men were moving this boat so painfully slowly that it was almost comical. They were all still snarling at us; one of them was still yelling. We had almost reached the ship, thank god, and the staff on the cruise had finally spotted us.

Just before we stepped onto the cruise ladder, the three men stopped us, forming a barrier between us and the ladder. They said we owed them 700 euros! They'd charged us another 100 euros just to take us to the boat! I was outraged. We protested, saying this wasn't the agreement. Before I could finish my point though, all three men were shouting again, their faces bright red. One of them had a hold of Mike's shoulders, whilst another was shaking the boat violently. It really seemed like they were going to hurt us, but then I noticed the oar lying on the rudder… Mike was shaking, and both men looked like they were about to push him into the sea. Without anyone noticing, I picked up the oar; it was very heavy. Thank God for my rudder experience because I just about managed to heave it up. The three men were faced the other way, now threatening Mike, who was desperately trying to get the men off as they were suffocating him. I took my chance; with all the strength I could muster I swung back the rudder and bought it crashing onto the men. With an almighty splash, the three men hit the water with cries of pain and shock.

"Look at you go! What did they do?!" Sophie said.

I explained how just after they fell into the water I noticed a police boat approaching; I thought I recognized the officers as the same ones who had seen us earlier, and I thought I was done for. I mean they'd obviously seen what I'd done - how could you miss that; everyone on the cruise decks was staring. But then the police boat just kept on going, completely passing us, and I could have sworn one of them winked at us as we boarded the cruise!

"Oh my god! That's amazing."

"A while afterwards we got a letter from the city", I said, "saying that they needed everyone involved, including the restaurant owners and all of the tourists…apparently we weren't the first people to get conned into paying hundreds of dollars from that Middle Eastern family and I was the first person to fight back! They even called me a hero!"

The Greatest Show on Earth

The cruise was my idea. Paul laughed when I suggested it – he said it sounded like the sort of thing his parents would do. But I'd always wanted to visit the Black Sea. My grandmother was from Batumi, on the Georgian coast. When I was little, sitting at the low table in the corner while she worked in her cramped little kitchen, she'd talk to me about the turquoise waters, the dark pebbled beaches, the hot summers and the sudden storms in winter that would sweep over the mountains and leave drifts of snow all the way down to the shoreline. I'd get so carried away listening that I'd forget to eat. She'd tap my plate.

'When food is in front of you, you should eat,' she said. 'Or someone else will take it.'

And she'd reach over and her short, rough fingers would pluck one of the steaming *khinkali* dumplings from my plate.

'What about this one?' said Paul. Once he had agreed to the trip he had thrown himself into researching the different cruise operators that plied the Black Sea. He leaned back in his chair, stretching. Paul was tall, athletic, with the same chestnut-colored hair that I had. In fact, we often got mistaken for siblings; though anyone Georgian instantly knew my family was from there, with my heavy brows and broad, angular features.

'It says they offer entertainment,' said Paul, pointing at the laptop screen.

'They all offer entertainment.'

'Yes, but according to their website, this company is "renowned for its avant-garde offerings."'

'Avant-garde? On a cruise ship?'

'That's what it says.'

You couldn't tell much about the show from the pictures. All I could see were shadowy figures moving through dim lighting.

'I don't know.'

'Fine. I know what will convince you.' He leaned over and navigated to a different part of the website. 'Their chef is Georgian.' There was a picture of a plate of *khinkali* dumplings. 'Just like your gran used to make.'

It seemed like a sign.

The cruise departed from Odessa. Our flight landed late, and Paul was determined to see the Potemkin Stairs before we boarded the ship. We peered out the taxi window at Odessa's tree-lined boulevards, at the bustling markets full of fresh fish. We went along cobbled streets and leaned towards the window as we passed the pale baroque edifice of the famous Opera Theatre.

The Potemkin stairs are near the harbor, so it shouldn't have been difficult to make our connection. But when the taxi pulled up there was such a crowd of people it was impossible to get a good view. I hauled my luggage behind me as we pushed through the crowd. Someone coming in the other direction bumped me, my satchel slipped from my shoulder and I leaned down to collect it. When I looked up, I couldn't see Paul.

I looked everywhere, but there was no sign of him. I felt a twinge of panic – a moment ago he'd been there. I called his name, but there was no reply.

Then I saw him, standing at the edge of the crowd. I hurried over.

'Isn't it incredible?' he said.

The stairs leaned away from us up the hill. They looked out of proportion somehow.

'It's an optical illusion,' said Paul. 'I read about it in the guidebook.'

He was right. The effect was eerie. Like the stairs might go on forever into the cold blue sky.

'We'd better hurry, or we'll miss the boat,' I said.

We made it, barely. After we found our cabin and unpacked we went to the dining room; neither of us had eaten since breakfast.

'Listen,' said Paul, as the waiter took our plates. 'We must already be far from shore.'

We stepped outside. He was right. The sea was as dark as the sky above us; it stretched on without interruption in every direction.

'What now?' I said.

'I know,' said Paul. 'We can go and see the show. You know, the famous avant-garde spectacle!'

I groaned.

'Come on, it'll be fun,' he said. He took my hand and started pulling me towards the theatre.

I thought back to the pictures I had seen on the laptop – the dark room, the heavy smoke. *At least it will be dark,* I thought. *If I fall asleep no one will notice.*

The theatre was enormous. I was shocked – I could hardly work out how such a large, sophisticated theatre had been put into a cruise ship. The strange thing about it was that the design of the theatre wasn't modern at all – it was all red curtains and gilt statuettes. The seats were a rich crimson color, rising steeply up into the auditorium like little blunt teeth. The auditorium was packed full of people. I was surprised; I thought more of the passengers would be out on deck. Their faces gleamed in the pale house lights. Almost like bodies in a morgue. As we took our seats a small woman in a dark green blouse leaned over to us.

'Are you excited?' she said. 'This is my third time on this cruise. They always put on such a great show.'

Her short, rough fingers gripped the back of my seat. She was already looking up at the stage, her eyes shining. There was something about her eagerness that was off-putting. I didn't like to think of her sitting there, just behind me. I felt like she might reach out and grab at me at any moment.

The lights went down.

About five minutes in, I was looking at Paul, trying to suppress a smile. The show didn't seem very avant-garde. It was a circus performance; it seemed to be about a young woman trying to escape the boredom of her own life. The story was charming and the performers were skillful, but I found my attention wandering. It was hard to see the faces of the rest of the audience, but I could see one man clearly, standing up the back, dressed in a black coat.

The show ended, and another began almost immediately. The woman in the green blouse laughed as oddly dressed acrobats clambered over each other to form a human tower. I glanced over my shoulder again and I noticed that the man in the black coat was gone. Then the lights cut out. Someone in the audience gasped. And then a noise so overpowering, like the spinning propellers of a helicopter right overhead.

The doors of the theatre crashed open. There were new performers, not like the acrobats, but dressed in dark clothes, their faces concealed. I looked at the woman in the green blouse. There was a weird smile on her face, but whether it was enjoyment or terror, I couldn't tell.

The performers were shouting in a language I couldn't understand. Russian? Ukrainian? It wasn't Georgian.

When the gunshots started I thought they were a stage effect. And then I thought, no, they must be blanks.

The only light in the theatre was a strange, dim red emergency light. Smoke was pouring into the auditorium. I felt Paul grab my hand.

'Let's go,' he said.

But I was frozen. I heard someone scream. Two men were dragging the woman in the green blouse from her seat. They dragged her up on stage and into the wings of the theatre. I don't remember hearing the gunshot, but Paul heard it. I only remember them carrying her body back out on stage and dropping it in front of the footlights. Blood pooled out across the stage.

Paul took a step forward, like he was about to say something, but I dragged him back down to his seat. The entire audience was silent.

Even as the hours dragged on, no one said anything. Even after days. We had no way of knowing how much time had passed but I knew it must have been days, at least. The men handed around food they must have taken from the dining rooms. Little plastic containers full of *khinkali* dumplings. Every bite I took I thought I wanted to throw up. We slept, sometimes, not knowing if it was day or night. One time, waking, I saw the smoke drifting across the stage again. This time, as it rolled over us, it had a strange taste. I shut my eyes. Further up in the auditorium I could hear someone shouting: 'Gas, it's gas.'

When I woke, I didn't know where I was. I wasn't in the theatre. This room wasn't shadowy and dark. It was bright – too bright. Someone leaned over me, a stranger in a mask, and I panicked, until I realized he was a nurse.

'Try to relax, I'll get the doctor.'

'I want to see Paul,' I said. 'Where's my husband?'

The nurse hurried away without saying anything at all. When the doctor finally arrived, she didn't answer any of my questions either.

'Where's Paul?' I asked again.

And I cried because it had been my idea to go on this cruise. It was all my fault. Without looking at me, the doctor said very quietly, like he wasn't supposed to be talking to me, 'He's alive.'

It was days until I saw Paul. He seemed like a stranger when he came in – like he was ten years older. His strong frame was stooped. There were even streaks of grey in his hair. He didn't seem to be hurt, but he didn't say anything when he sat down. We didn't hold each other. We didn't even hold hands.

'We need to leave,' I said, finally. 'We just need to forget all this and go home. I don't care about anything else.'

Paul took a piece of paper out of his pocket, slowly unfolded it, and handed it to me.

It was a document, written in Russian and English. It seemed to be a kind of legal waiver. We were free to leave, it said, as long as we signed the form declaring we had freely participated in an avant-garde interactive performance, and we were satisfied with our experience.

I tried not to think of the woman in the green blouse. Her rough fingers are so much like my grandmother's.

'Give me a pen,' I said, and I signed.

The Haunting

The grass is still damp from the overnight rain, even now in the late morning when Mari and a few others walk slowly from the common room of the nursing home towards the pavilion. A nurse guides the small group, not one of them younger than ninety.

'Mari, maybe you'd like to share with everyone the story you told me yesterday,' says the nurse, Cleo, as she arranges the chairs.

Mari nods. 'Yes. I was thinking about it last night. There were things I forgot to tell you. Terrible things. Things I thought that I would never forget.'

'Don't scare everyone, now,' says Cleo, smiling.

'This happened when I was very young,' Mari began.

An old man walks towards them, older even than any of the people sitting in the pavilion. Hunched over with age, he almost resembles a gargoyle from a cathedral spire. Cleo pauses, offering to help, but the old man waves her away and takes a seat with the rest of the group and swivels his pale, watery blue eyes towards Mari.

'Are you new here?' one of them asks.

The old man seems to nod.

'You're so familiar,' says Mari. 'But I can't remember from where, I'm sorry. Maybe I'm forgetting faces now.'

'Tell us the story, Mari,' says one of the old men. 'Cleo says it's a good one.'

Mari nods, but her eyes don't leave the face of the stranger. 'As I was saying, this all happened a very long time ago.'

'I was on holiday, in Genoa. Bill and I had just got engaged. We didn't see much of the city. We were so happy just being together that it was enough to walk along the shore. I didn't care that we were missing out on seeing the Palazzi dei Rolli.

It became our habit to go down to the harbor and watch the sunrise, listen to the gulls and all the fishermen starting work. This morning we walked farther than usual, around to the dry docks, where the ships are repaired and built. There was one ship in particular that caught our attention. It was a new ocean liner, quite small. It was designed to take fewer passengers, but it would offer a luxury service. The design was cutting edge for the time, in particular its double-skinned hull.

I remember seeing it half-complete, hanging out of the water. Like a skeleton. There were two workmen arguing on shore. They seemed very upset. But of course they were speaking in Italian – I couldn't understand them.

Bill and I got married that summer. We didn't have any ideas about our honeymoon, but one morning

Bill opened the newspaper and there was an advertisement for the ship. Its maiden voyage, from Southampton to New York. It seemed perfect.

It was extraordinary to see the boat completed. It spanned three decks, and where most cruise ships of the time were bulky, like a tall building turned on its side, this ship was sleek, almost like a superyacht, except no one had built one of them before. It was the first of its kind. It balanced on the water like a knife, and its black hull gleamed like polished marble.

Those first nights – I don't think I've ever danced so much! The band played late into the night and most of us on board were young and there to enjoy ourselves. But there was one man who wasn't having fun. He wouldn't dance, he only sat there in the corner, drinking. He was a crooked, sour-faced man. He had dark circles under his blue eyes, like he hadn't slept in weeks. His clothes were expensive, but unclean. I remember thinking he must have been a manual worker, because his hands were covered in tiny white scars. Everyone thought it best to keep away from him, but I made the mistake of talking to him one night. He claimed to have been an engineer who worked on the construction of the ship and he told me this nasty little story about punishing a worker who'd made mistakes during the ship's construction. I could smell the alcohol on his breath, so I didn't take him seriously. It just seemed like the ravings of an unpleasant drunk.

The thing is, I think part of the reason we all danced so late is that none of us wanted to go to bed. Because as soon as you went to bed all you could listen to were the sounds of the ship at night. The wind and the waves and the creaking of the hull. These were all normal sounds, but there were other things. Voices. At first I thought it must be my mind playing tricks on me, but when I finally told Bill what I heard, he said that he had heard it too. A friend we had made on board, Lucy, said maybe it was a ghost. People were much more superstitious back then, it didn't seem like a strange thing to think.

But then every night we'd get dressed up and we'd go to the ballroom, where the musicians were waiting for us in their evening suits. And the music would start and we'd get to our feet and dance and dance and forget all about the voices.

I can still remember the feeling of being out in the Atlantic, so far from everything. Nothing but the ocean for miles, dark cloud rolling across the endless sky, the gentle pitching of the ship whenever we met a wave.

A week into the voyage, the strange voices became harder to ignore. We could tell the crew members were edgy – they were hearing the voices as well. And not just voices. There were knocking sounds all over the ship, in different places every night. Like something was trying to claw through the walls.

Every night we'd keep going up to the ballroom, but no one danced anymore. Our friend Lucy whispered to us that she was cancelling her return ticket. She wasn't alone. The only person who didn't seem upset was the drunkard engineer. He sat at the bar every night, drinking and laughing to himself. We thought about cancelling our ticket, but we were a young married couple; we didn't have much money. Our return ticket was our only way home.

The night before we arrived in New York we heard screaming. It was clear, but distant. As if you could hear someone screaming from just over there, inside the nursing home. The moment we landed there was nearly a stampede to get off the ship.

We only spent a few days in New York. It wasn't as long as we'd hoped, but Bill had to get back to work. The city must be so different today, but even then it was an extraordinary place. I'd never seen so many people all at once. And the skyscrapers!

It was almost enough to make us forget about how strange our journey had been. By the time we were getting back on board the ship, we were feeling like maybe somehow we had imagined the whole thing. That first night, the ballroom was nearly empty. Even some of the musicians had decided not to come back on the return voyage, and those that were left played to drown out the screaming. On the third night, we were woken, the noise was like a loud, dull thud, different to anything we had heard so far. Bill ran out of the cabin. When he finally came back, he was pale as a sheet. "Don't go out there," he said. "A boiler exploded. There were six men in the room. They're all dead."

I went looking for the drunkard who'd haunted the bar on our outward voyage. He had claimed to be an engineer working on the ship, so I wondered if he knew something about the boiler. I couldn't find him. I guessed he must have stayed on shore in New York.

The closer we got to home, the fainter the screaming sounds became, until by the time we were disembarking at Southampton we could hardly hear them at all. They weren't even like screams anymore. Just a faint, desperate whine.

I kept hearing stories about that ship as the years went by. Accidents, people jumping overboard for no reason. People said that it was cursed. One day, Bill looked up from reading the newspaper and told me the ship was gone. It had been coming into port in Hamburg it hit an old mine, and sunk. No one died, thankfully. Still, I was sad. Even though that trip had been the strangest month of my life, it was my honeymoon. That beautiful, state-of-the-art ship. Gone.

Only that wasn't the end of it. When they dragged it up from the sea floor and dismantled it, when they peeled back the double-skinned hull, they found two bodies. Skeletons. Trapped between the outer and the inner hull. And sure enough, two riveters had disappeared during the construction of the ship all those years ago in Genoa. Finally, they had been found.'

Mari breaks off. The group turns towards the stranger who had joined them. He's laughing.

'I'm sorry,' he says. 'I'm sorry to laugh, it's just…'

Laughter shakes his ancient frame. His hands wipe away tears of mirth.

'I do know you from somewhere,' says Mari.

'It was a long time ago. I drink less, now. Back then I drank to drown out their screams but now…

now you see all I can do is laugh. I remember you from the ballroom. The honeymooners.' The old man leans forward in his seat. 'Do you know how perfectly my designs needed to be executed for that ship to succeed? And all the time I was surrounded by lazy scroungers who refused to pull their weight. Those two were the worst of the lot. It was easy to lure them into the space between the hulls. "Last minute welding," I said. "I'll pay you double." They believed it. Well, it was true in a way. As soon as they were inside I had the hatch welded shut.'

The crowd of old people murmur in discomfort. 'Get away from us,' says one woman. 'You're cursed, like that ship.'

Mari sits very still, an expression of horrified revulsion on her face. The old man shrugs. 'I'm too old for jail,' he says. 'And I already know hell.'

He lifts his black hat in farewell. They watch him walk away across the damp grass. Cleo, the nurse, watches him anxiously. Without warning, the old man lifts his face to the overcast sky, and screams.

'The same sound,' Mari whispers to herself. 'The same voice.'

Forever on Board

Cruising the Caribbean was an annual tradition for Jennifer Jones. Mrs. Jones, or simply "Miss Jenny" to those closest to her, was about to turn eighty, a milestone that she meant to celebrate on board her favorite luxury cruise liner, even if her weary bones now protested when she climbed the steps from the dock, or hurried to join her fellow passengers for afternoon tea on one of the many pleasant verandas which overlooked the oceanic expanse. In fact, given that she had made this trip nigh thirty years, *everyone* on board was close to her, down to the most marginal of staff. And if you were a first-time passenger, she made *sure* you knew who she was before long, because Miss Jenny was incredibly proud of her status as "Queen of the Caribbean".

Today the ship would make one of its many ports of call at the island of Saint Martin, but Miss Jenny was not interested in debarking. Oh, many years ago docking had been her absolute favorite aspect of any Caribbean voyage. It used to bring a shiver down her spine to think of the mysteries and particularities of each port and island, the different traditions and cuisines which awaited the traveler, or the architectural wonders and grand curving avenues which held their own reclusive, personal charms. But this was all old news. At this point in her cruising career, Miss Jenny was content to wait on board while the "kids", as she was apt to call them, had their frolics. For what Miss Jenny truly enjoyed now was kicking back with a dry martini, watching the soft blue waters which stretched to the meridian, and thinking of nothing at all.

Miss Jenny rattled the ice in her martini glass and looked about her. The deck was now deserted. Gulls wheeled over the ocean and there was a strong scent of salt in the air; the kind of nautical details that made her feel she had arrived at last, to what Herman Melville once deemed man's last frontier: the darker margins of the sea. She leaned back in the reclining chair and sighed, a sound that, if you knew Miss Jenny, meant total contentment.

"Miss Jenny, mam, can I get you anything else?" asked a striking, middle-aged man with a French accent.

"Oh, monsieur Raphael, you startled me! I thought I was quite alone here." Miss Jenny looked at Raphael, whom she knew somewhat less than the other crew members. He was a new hand that season, but his bearing had instantly won her over from the time she stepped on board.

"I'm sorry. I didn't want to disturb your…reverie? Is that the right word?"

"Quite so. No need to worry about your English around a woman like me. I am quite simple, though you might think otherwise. Why, I'm just an old gal from greater Tallahassee…tell me, where are you from, Paris? Oh, do please tell me you…"

"Miss Jenny, it's no matter where I'm from. It's of no… *consequence*. I wanted to talk about you." He gave her his most charming smile, which at that moment looked the very definition of a viper's grin.

But, as we all know, vipers hold their own allure. Miss Jenny, feeling like a young girl all over again, replied somewhat breathlessly,   "Monsieur Raphael…why…what do you want to know of me?"

"Why is it that you never go with the others onto the islands? Day after day, I've seen you sitting here. Yes, I've looked in on you at times, but I've always…refrained…from disturbing you. You look so peaceful. I've just watched you and thought to myself "why, she does not look a day over fifty. Fine legs, lustrous hair…why does she not join the others and be gallivant?" Yes, Raphael would like to know this."

"Well Raphael, it's just that I've already seen all and done all. At this point in my life, I don't think there is much left for me to experience really. What pleasure I get is now within myself, thinking about things, about memories…or just talking to others…like you. I guess that's why I still come on this cruise every year."

"Miss Jenny, you can't really think such nonsense. There are surely some things you have yet to experience". Raphael gave her another of his venomous smiles, which contained equal hints of malice and charm.

"Why, Raphael…."

Witnesses would later say they had observed Raphael leaning over the old woman, too close for comfort. *He leaned over her crookedly, all limbs, like a gangly spider over its prone, web-shrouded prey.*

That night, when all the passengers gathered for dinner after the outing on Saint Martin, the elderly Miss Jenny was nowhere to be seen. Usually, a missing guest would cause little to no stir, it not being remarkable that they would prefer to spend the mealtime in their cabin. But Miss Jenny was different. She was the star of the buffet, carousing from table to table telling stories about past trips that her fellow passengers would feign interest in hearing. When she did not show up that night, there was some grumbling about how she must be very ill, or else in bad spirits to miss such an opportunity to "shine".

When she did not show up for breakfast the next morning, worry amongst the passengers mounted. And at afternoon tea, when there was still no sign of the venerable Miss Jenny, several of the passengers decided to pay a visit to her cabin, just to make sure nothing was truly amiss. They knocked and knocked, but there was no response from Miss Jenny. One passenger, a heavy-set woman with curly hair the texture and color of old iron, thought to go immediately to the head of staff and report the disappearance of Miss Jenny. Something had to be wrong! No sign of her for an entire day, and now no answer from the barrage of knocks on her cabin door. Where could she be? Had she actually, once and for all, decided to get off at the last port of call without anyone having noticed? Oh, poor Miss Jenny!

It was soon concluded that the last person to see and talk to Miss Jenny was the new steward, Mr. Raphael Barthes. But when pressed, Raphael could only give vague statements about his last encounter with Miss Jenny.

"Well, you see, I spoke to her a bit on the deck yesterday afternoon…. she was a bit drunk. Yes, very drunk! I stopped to see if she was ok. I swear, an old lady like that, drunk and alone on a ship. Anything could happen!"

Raphael said all of this in his exaggerated French accent, which seemed peculiar and contrived when coupled with his extensive English vocabulary, or at least that is what the heavy-set passenger, Mrs. Montgomery, the now de facto "head of search", thought.

"Where did she go then? What was she doing when you last saw her, Mr. Barthes?"

"Why, she was leaning against the railing, peering into the water. But she looked quite steady at that point. Really."

Everything did not quite add up. Especially when other members of the crew reported seeing Raphael and Miss Jenny leaving the deck together. The passengers, along with the ship's management, decided to contact the authorities at the port of Saint Martin. The ship was redirected and made to return to the harbor of said island. There was now a kind of bubbling hysteria amongst those on the ship, as the disappearance of Miss Jenny pointed to the possibility of foul play. Everyone had begun to suspect the sneaky Frenchman, Raphael, and he was now rarely seen on deck due to the suspicious looks cast his way.

The authorities turned out to be of little or no help. They did not seem interested in the case, and merely suggested that a little money to line their pockets would "help" them begin inquiries. In the end, a group of five police officers reluctantly scoured the ship after much coaxing from the crew, but no trace of Miss Jenny was found. It was as if she had vanished into thin air.

Due to her disappearance the remainder of the cruise was cut short. The crew decided to return immediately to Miami, where a report would be made in full, and an investigation hopefully ensued.

To everyone's surprise, during the last leg of their return voyage the heavy-set woman with the wiry hair was often seen carousing with the top suspect, monsieur Raphael. Where she had before seemed hostile to the man's very presence, she now soaked it up. They were even seen holding hands once, under a Cuban moon pregnant with portent. When the ship finally reached US soil, the newly smitten couple hurried off board before the authorities had time to detain them. To everyone's great dismay, it would seem the suspect, *and* the lead prosecutor, had made a run for it.

    The disappearance of old Miss Jenny was never solved, and Raphael and Mrs. Montgomery are at large to this very day. Strange things are now reported on the ship frequented by Miss Jenny. There are grumblings among the crew of a faint shimmering on the edge of their visions, though they can never say for certain if it is indeed the haunting of Miss Jenny or merely their nerves. But what is most poignant about this most peculiar of tales is the fact that passengers that have since slept in Miss Jenny's favored cabin, number 109, all describe the same supernatural occurrence: often, in the dead of night, a woman's frail voice will issue from the ventilation ducts which supply the room with air. Something like a stuttering death's rattle takes greater and greater form until it becomes distinctly *human*. This voice will never denounce cold murder, but only bore the current occupant with banal tales of her many times spent cruising.

"I cruised the Caribbean nearly every year of my adult life. You were still wearing diapers when I was rubbing elbows at Captain Hook's Rum Bar… "

Finding Lasting Love

My name is Dennie and it all begins tomorrow. Packing the luggage is no cakewalk and even though I've been preparing for weeks I currently have problems to keep a clear head. I need to know exactly what I have to pack and what I have to leave at home. I have just read that I mustn't take any bottles or groceries with me.

The cruise starts in Italy. There are no real cruises starting in Germany except river cruises like they have on the Danube or Rhine, but they are exclusively for retirees.

My vacation on a cruise ship begins tomorrow in the evening. It's an enormous vessel with several swimming pools and lots of restaurants. The idea to book a cruise came to my mind when I met an old friend. She had already spread the news on Facebook that she had finally found her dream man.

Life can be that beautiful! After ten years of online dating my overweight female friend has finally found a boyfriend. He must be a rich guy; now I know how much such a cruise trip costs. My trip had cost over five thousand Euros, but my friend's voyage must have been even more expensive. My thoughts are wandering between packing and posh guys, cocktails and toiletries. It's better to have plenty of them. Tampons and shampoos fortunately don't weigh a lot. I hear the doorbell ringing. Who might that be, I have no time!

"Hello, Andrea! What a surprise!"

"Hello Dennie, I just wanted to say a last time hello before you'll start your cruise trip tomorrow. May I introduce you to my fiancé. This is Bobo from Manila."

"I'm pleased to meet you"

"Hello!"

"Does he also speak English?"

"He speaks English very well. After all he had worked on the cruise ship where I met him. He was a waiter there. He is quite a capable man!"

The Vegan Passenger

In hindsight, if it's worth anything, I must say that I had a fantastic cruise. The moon over Salem Harbor was just spectacular, and I can recall in my mind's eye how the water looked like an unblemished mirror. I almost felt like one of those hapless women in a Lovecraftian horror tale, transfixed by otherworldly powers. I leaned on the starboard railing and thought about my life up to that point, all my trials, all my joys.

Despite all warnings, I began the cruise alone. The fact is, I had no one to accompany me. All my girlfriends hate cruises. But my primary aim was just to enjoy myself, relax, and experience something fresh. Where I come from, novel things are not really a matter of course. It's a pretty stale little town, and the only thing we have for entertainment are dive bars and dollar stores. So, you see, a cruise is a big deal to me.

I have to admit something though. There was another reason that spurred me to take this cruise, and it is something that goes beyond just pleasure. This cruise, called the "Spar Cruise", is also a wellness retreat. I've been suffering from obesity nearly my entire adult life, and diets have never stuck. I feel like I just get bigger and bigger, year after year. As soon as I go off a diet, I balloon right up. I wanted a program that induced action, which eclipsed diets and resulted in a lifestyle change. I had tried everything up until that point, from YouTube videos to old aerobics tapes. No, something substantial had to happen, and a wellness cruise seemed like just the thing to kickstart a new life.

    Since this was an Asian themed cruise, they had a vegetarian Indian restaurant on board. I have to admit, the first day I skipped my plans to begin a nutritional diet. There was just too much delicious food in sight; I couldn't help myself. I figured that by being on a wellness cruise, one didn't really need a plan. The results were sure to come of themselves. What I discovered soon after boarding, and what I came to like most about the ship I was on, was the fact that they had two or more themed restaurants, giving me a variety of choices. The Japanese and the Indian restaurants are the ones I vividly recall. The cakes and pastries in the Indian restaurant were made with real whip cream, not the imitation powder stuff. The food was excellent, that's the least I can say. The first evening I ate entirely too much, and afterwards slept for almost thirteen hours. I only woke up because my friend from the Weight Watchers program wanted to chat, and my ringtone was loud enough to cut through my heavy, sugar-induced slumber.

"Girl, how are you doing out there in the water?"

"Honestly, not so good. I ate *so* much last night, like a pig."

"You know what the Weight Watchers manual says: start a meat-free diet when you are at a point in your life when you are happily distracted. Isn't that what a cruise ship is all about? Distraction?"

"You are probably right Sally, but it just feels so damn hard. You know, that first step."

"You got this girl. I believe in you."

I did have to admit this was sound advice. I could use all the distractions on board so I wouldn't be white-knuckling and battling the cravings all the time. So, from that day on, I started to eat at a more reasonable pace and used all the restaurants and their attendant buffets are smartly as I could. I also made it a habit to get a full body oil massage from one of those very friendly Bangladeshi masseurs, whose hands were not only gentle but slightly erotic. It really helped with my stress levels, and besides, I've read time and time again that a massage burns calories.

My only complaint at the time was the fact that most of the male crew members seemed to stare at me. Well, maybe it was my imagination, but I don't think so. I caught them many times out of the corner of my eye. I know I'm overweight, but I'm no freak. I started to become a little self-conscious and made sure never to wear my G-string when people were about.

On the third day out from port I started to explore the vessel more and more to see what kind of healthy activities were available. I was talking to another passenger, an elderly lady that was on board in order to practice her yoga skills, and she informed me that they had a cooking class for vegans, and that it was all the rage among the "in" crowd on the ship. And what's more, she told me that the man leading the course was a strapping gentleman of Indian heritage, and that he had all the ladies weak in the knees. I thought to myself that this would be the perfect solution: having fun, eating vegetarian, getting thin as a rake, all in the company of a charming man to boot. This was really what I had been waiting for; now my journey to self-improvement had really begun.

Soon, I started to only order vegetarian food at the Indian restaurant. Even all the tasty morsels on the buffet couldn't tempt me. It was almost like I had become a really devoted vegan, out of the blue! I became a regular at this Indian restaurant, and my absolute favorite dish was the vegan-vegetable soup. I ate it in bucketloads, not only because it was healthy, but I felt free from the sin of eating live beings. I was doing something good for myself *and* the environment for a change.

Towards the end of the cruise, I asked the Indian chef at the restaurant why the soup always tasted so incredibly good. I really wanted the recipe, for how was I going to live without it! Giving me a somewhat sheepish grin, he said that the secret of his recipe was that it contained chicken broth and lots of lard. He said the chicken broth was the real *spice*, an element of the animal kingdom that no vegetable could duplicate.

After hearing that, I had a real nervous breakdown. I mean, here I thought I was eating something healthy and soulful, but it was the same old crap I had been stuffing myself with for years, full of fat and animal products. It was almost too much for me to bear. I left the buffet that night with a heavy heart, for I had felt truly devoted to this new lifestyle. But it had all been a sham, a mirage. I was still the same pig I had always been.

I locked myself in my cabin for the remainder of the trip and refused to see anyone. I was so shocked by the chef's secret that I ordered pizzas and had them delivered to my door: *large, triple-cheese, thanks*. I gorged myself on donuts and processed sweets from the vending machines, eating to my heart's content, trying to drown my memory of the "vegan" soup in a deluge of sugar. I couldn't believe it. I went from a vegan with monk-like discipline to a slob gorging herself on fast-food overnight! I bet the crew didn't even notice the pounds I packed on, for they had miraculously stopped ogling me, but the scale sure did when I got back home.

The Tourist Guide

Carlos was born and raised in Veracruz, Mexico, but he has been living in New Jersey for over a decade. Since he had an accident, and no one could help take care of him; he decided to go back to his country and live there with his family. Now he is a tour guide for mostly American tourists in Cancun. When the cruise ships come there are virtually thousands of English speaking tourists who not only want to see the beaches and restaurants; but are keen to explore the countryside and what the surrounding culture has to offer.

Carlos accepts group tours as well as individual tourists. He is quite popular and made himself a name as a knowledgeable guide, who has gained a small fan community on various online travel platforms. The tours usually start early in the morning and last until late afternoon. Many tourists wonder how Carlos speaks English without an accent. He tells them a little about himself, but that usually leads to more private questions. Carlos is not oblivious; for each question he has prepared a perfect answer. This is something he had learned in the US.

Table Sharing

Mr. and Mrs. Bloom did not usually do this sort of thing. Mr. William Bloom was a retired toxicologist of some renown, having worked at Cambridge performing outlandish experiments on zebrafish, and Mrs. Louise Bloom was a retired English teacher with a penchant for leather-bound classics. They were both deeply cultured; their usual vacations involved forays to famous museums and trendy popup galleries, or else visits to one Michelin star restaurant or another across the continent. But a *cruise*? Out of the question! That is why they found things a little uncomfortable as they made their way onto the gigantic cruiser that would take them on a tour around the Mediterranean, from Gibraltar to Greece and beyond.

"Why, William, it looks like this ship is practically *swarming* with people. Look at them all! And all so loud and obnoxious, like they had never been on a vacation before."

"I know Louise", Mr. Bloom replied, "you would almost think that the ship had been overbooked. I really hope it does not feel this way once everyone disperses to their cabins. You know how I hate crowds."

The Blooms made their way down the gaudily carpeted corridor, directed to their own private cabin by one of the helpful, albeit overly cheerful, crew staff. Once they get to their room, they relieved themselves of their personal belongings and stretch out on the king-sized bed, welcoming the peace and quiet after the initial rush to get onboard the ship and settled.

"I beg the food is at least good, or tolerable. I hope we have our own table by the window. That's what I really want: my own dining table so I don't have to mingle."

"William, you really are something else. The whole *point* of a cruise is to mingle and get to know others. I know I am looking forward to that. But yes, I am also looking forward to some quiet so that I can finish up this mystery novel I have been working on."

"I'm sure you will get the opportunity my love. Right now, I can't even think about books. I'm very hungry. Let's go see if we can be seated in the dining hall, though the hour is a bit early.

Mrs. Bloom stretched and yawned. She thought to herself, *I just know William is going to make this a miserable trip. He can't stand being "one of the proletariats." Sigh.*

"Ok dear. Let's go get some food and maybe meet some of the others." *Maybe*.

When they got to the dining hall, which stretched dizzyingly as far as the eye could see, they noticed that every single chair was already occupied. There was a din of garbled voices, an array of languages and dialects that all seemed to merge into one riotous wall of sound. Mr. Bloom was visibly assaulted; even Mrs. Bloom, the cheerful one, was taken aback. Where could they possibly sit? Must they dine separately?

One of the serving staff hurried over and explained the situation. The ship was indeed overbooked, its capacity stretched to the limits. On account of this, a special dining area was being opened for the remaining guests unable to find adequate seating.

"This way. It's just down the corridor and to the left. I promise, you will not be disappointed. You may even find it cozier and more intimate than this one", said the staff member, a young brunette who soon introduced herself as the senior hostess. "If anything is wrong or not to your satisfaction, only tell your server to inform me. I will be sure to make any amends necessary."

"Oh great, more *intimate*", William grumbled as they were shown the way to the alternative dining hall.

They were eventually seated at a round table that, as they will later be informed, would be their permanent place of dining for the remainder of the cruise. It was pleasant enough, with a view of the sea, but what irked them, especially Mr. Bloom, was the fact that they shared it with strangers, a German man and woman. And what's more, they were not only strangers, but incredibly obnoxious strangers. The German couple barely introduced themselves, Mr. and Mrs. Bloom only catching that their surname was "Weber", and proceeded to speak loudly in High German throughout the entire meal, hardly pausing their verbal tirade between mouthfuls. Mr. and Mrs. Bloom couldn't converse, for they were drowned out by the rough German consonants and deep vowels.

What added to our British couple's distress was the fact that they had to spend *every* mealtime with these two buffoons. Mr. and Mrs. Bloom soon found out that the Germans' initial behavior was no outlier; they spoke wildly *every* time they ate, gesturing and splashing beer about like philistines. It was almost too much to bear.

And to make matters worse, the Blooms were cabin neighbors with this disagreeable couple. In the wee hours of the morning they were prone to hearing the Germans argue in their harsh tongue, or else have impassioned sex which the thin walls serving as partitions did little to conceal.

All these auditory offenses came to a head one day when Mr. and Mrs. Bloom decided to spend the day poolside, in an effort to derive whatever relaxation this horrible cruise had to offer. Instead they found that this selfsame German couple had proceeded to reserve not two, but *six* chairs of prime real-estate by draping towels across them.

"This is just too much, really", said Mr. Bloom. Mrs. Bloom, despite her best efforts, couldn't help but agree with her contrary husband.

"I know William. I know. This is out of hand. But what are we to do? They are not exactly doing anything *wrong* according to the book…"

"Maybe not according to the book. But I have had it with these two. I think I have a trick or two up my sleeve that might just *cure* the situation."

William stared off into the distance, reminding Louise of those times when he was absorbed in his work – deep in the annals of his beloved toxicology.

"Now, if we can just secure some potatoes that have a green hue about them. Of course, I can devise my own mortar and pestle, that is no matter. Louise, please, bear with me. Do you think you can manage to somehow make your way into the kitchen and get a bucketful?"

"Are you sure you want to do this William? We could get in a lot of trouble. My god, you are talking about poisoning someone!"

"Don't worry. I will mix it in such a fashion that it will only make them very sick. They will think it's mere salmonella. Hey, it may even afford us a few dinners in peace. Nobody will know the better. Just get me those potatoes."

The next night at dinner, amidst one of the Germans' now infamous drunken outbursts, Mr. Bloom stealthily produced a small tincture from his vest pocket and tried tapping a portion of the vile powder onto the Caesar salads of the unsuspecting Germans. But a sudden draft from the antique ventilation system sent the fine powder into the room, out amongst the other diners in an inconspicuous cloud.

"Stupid is what stupid does", exclaimed Mr. Bloom. He hurriedly placed the tincture back into his pocket and looked down at his plate, his face now turning a deep crimson.

"Harold, what did you just do? I thought…"

"Nothing Louise. Just eat."

The next morning, both Mr. and Mrs. Bloom woke up feeling incredibly ill. Though they had both only drank one glass of wine the previous night, they were startled to find they were nursing the worst hangovers of their lives.

"It's the solanine. We must have inhaled it as well. Lucky for us I produced an antidote in case of any mishap. Such are the joys of alchemy."

"But William, what about the other passengers? This is a nightmare. I knew you should not have gone through with this crazy plan."

That night, they were one of only three couples in the reserve dining hall, where before there had been twenty or more. The Germans were nowhere to be seen. The serving staff cast them dark, suspicious looks, and the other couple's avoided eye contact with them. The Blooms were becoming more and more agitated, though Mr. Bloom was sure no one had seen his move.

"William, we must try to disembark at the next port. We can make up some excuses! Anything. We will find a way back to England, be it by sea or land."

"I think you are right dear. There is no telling how potent that solanine mixture was. I mean, I *have* been retired for some time."

As they made their way back to their cabin to prepare for their eventual departure they heard moans of agony emanating from every cabin door they passed

"Harold, the door is locked from the outside! Come here. This is impossible."

"Damn it to all hell, I'll have to call ship security", William said as he picked up the receiver. There was no dial tone.

"The line is dead."

Through their door, the Blooms heard a wild laugh that was abruptly cut short by a fit of coughing and gagging.

"Herr Bloom, never underestimate the ingenuity and determination of a German engineer. Even a sick, drunk one!"

The Captain's Compartment

Why do I always bring so much with me? You would think that I would've learned my lesson by now. I never need this much stuff! A single mom of two should know better.

    Karen stood on the dock and waited her turn while the line of passengers slowly made their way on board the ship. This was her fourth time taking a cruise in as many years, but still, the compulsion to bring *everything* and the kitchen sink had not been curbed. She would spend days packing, checking off an extensive list of must-have items only to add a slew of unnecessary things to her Samsonite travel bag right before heading off. But this time she had really overdone it. She could barely lift her luggage off the ground, and it took both arms and significant effort to even get its wheels to roll. What was she going to do?

Karen looked at the scene around her. Passengers moseyed or stood patiently in the midday heat, all of them dressed in their Caribbean finest: flip-flops and cargo shorts, the men in their token Hawaiian print shirts, or else women in colorful summer dresses and oversized, designer sunglasses which reflected the hard sun. She was on the verge of asking an aging gentleman in a velour blazer for help when she spotted a man whose presence seemed to part the crowd with no words spoken. He was evidently part of the senior crew, or perhaps the captain himself. He walked with an air of nautical assuredness and his hat was adorned with the exquisite gold leafing peculiar to his profession. As if sensing her distress and need, this lofty specimen was made directly for her. He was quite young, tall, and solidly built. He sported a wavy brown pompadour haircut and his green eyes sparkled like smashed jade.

"How do you do, miss? I'm the captain of this mighty vessel. My name is William Strobeck. You may call me Bill."

Karen took his extended hand and at once noticed how cold and free of perspiration his grip was, even in the blistering heat. She was taken aback by presence but managed to blurt out, "I'm Karen. Nice to meet you captain."

"Please. As I said, just Bill. One should be on most familiar terms with the man who pilots their ship, wouldn't you say? Now, I see that you are alone and possess an *incredibly* large bag. Can I help you on board with that?" The smile he flashed her held a note of mischief and anticipation.

"Oh, captain…Bill, that's very kind of you. But I think I can manage it myself. It's not so heavy as it looks".

Karen wondered, despite his seemingly Samaritan intentions, why he had bothered to approach her amongst this crowd of people. Did she really look so helpless?

"Nonsense. Please, this way. Follow me". The captain pulled her luggage bag behind him effortlessly and shouted for the crowd to kindly make way. Karen followed in his wake, bypassing the other passengers waiting their turn. She noticed some of them cast her angry, irritating looks.

Captain Bill Strobeck looked back at her and asked, "Now, which cabin number are you assigned to? Ah, never mind all that. We can take your baggage directly to the captain's compartment. I have *plenty* of room in my spacious suite. Just you wait and see."
Too startled to contradict him, Karen followed the fine form of the young captain through the still desolate halls of the ship.

Later, Karen will claim that what happened within the captain's compartment was anything but clear. She recalled that the captain wooed her gently; that he called her a "mature flower" and claimed she was the most beautiful passenger he had ever had the luck to meet. He offered her a drink, that much she remembers. But after that, everything seemed to meld into one miasma of passion she had thought long dead in the years after the birth of her children and subsequent divorce. When she next woke, she was in the cabin she had originally been assigned, and all that remained of the captain was a small skeleton key with a tag attached to it that read: *Captain's Compartment*.

Two months later Karen booked another cruise, making sure that it was the same ship in hopes of once again meeting the mysterious captain that she had spent one heady, impassioned afternoon with.

This time around, she made sure to pack and bring *two* large suitcases, so as to get the young captain's attention if he yet again made an appearance on the dock prior to boarding. Before long, Karen saw his pearly whites flashing in the sun, and his pompadour bouncing proudly above even the tallest of passengers. Again, he singled her out of the vast crowd and made a line for her. Karen waited, feeling weak in the knees, her heart aching.

"Why, how do you do….Karen. Say, can I help you with your luggage? You appear overburdened. I have just the place you can keep them."

After another afternoon that passes in a kind of carnal blur, Karen had dinner in the main dining hall where she struck up a conversation with another woman her age, also a single divorcee, Miss Amy Sanders of Pensacola, Florida.

"Amy, you would not imagine the luck I have had… the afternoon I have just had." Karen looked dreamily out upon the sea as she struggles to recall just exactly *what* happened. "I think I could be falling in love."

"Really? With who?"

"Why, you wouldn't believe it, but it's…the *captain*".

"You don't mean captain William!?"

Karen looked startled and replied, "Yes, captain William Strobeck. Captain Bill. Do you know him?"

"Of course, I know him". Amy stood up for a second, but lowered herself again and then leaned across the table so that only Karen could hear, "We had an affair last year. He would always offer to keep my luggage in his cabin, though I would never see him again after the initial encounter".

Karen shook her head. "My god, this is so strange. I don't know what to say. What could he possibly want by keeping our luggage in his compartment?

Amy smiled like a siren. "Mine is there now; I have the key". She produced the strange looking skeleton key while Karen widened her eyes in shock.
Amy looked around. "Say, Karen, let's both sneak in there tonight and have a look. There is something fishy about all this."

When Karen and Amy made their way to the captain's compartment, the halls were dead, the hour well past midnight. Karen fit the eccentric key into the lock and turned ever so slowly, as not to wake the captain if he was by chance in the compartment. The key wouldn't turn. She tried again, with a little more force, but still couldn't get the lock to spring. She rattled the key around a bit when suddenly the door was thrown wide. The captain stood in the opening wearing only a green satin robe, pulled loosely about himself and tied a private eye of some renown from Chicago. Karen felt like it was a prime opportunity to tell her story, for she had by that time become suspicious of the captain's intentions. Something just did not sit well with her.

"Miss Karen, why do you think he is hiding something? What are you suspicious of?"

"I don't know Mr. Clark, but first it was Amy, and now me. And always the compartment and this strange forgetfulness afterward. Amy claimed similarly."

"Ok. It does sound strange, to say the least. How about we both go and check out what is really behind his door? I have means of gaining entry, and I have a clear mind. We will solve this together."

Karen directed him down the winding passageway to the captain's compartment, and the detective set to work with his specialized lock picking utensils.

hastily at the waist. He smiled at them both, his green eyes piercing.

"What do you two think you are doing, especially at this hour of the night? It can only mean one thing…"

He held his hand out toKaren and with one nasty, glaring look, dismissed Amy. She retreated down the hall submissively, not even bothering to look over her shoulder at what was transpiring between Karen and Bill. Karen found herself drawn into the cabinet seemingly against her will, as if she has been unwittingly drugged.

Karen woke in the same state she always found herself in after her rendezvous with the charming captain. Her head felt heavy and her thoughts clouded, recollection of the night spent in the captain's arms but a fleeting image, an impression dancing at the edge of consciousness.

The following night at dinner she happened to strike up a conversation with a man who turned out to be

When he finally pried open the heavy door, the compartment was empty, though the smell of the captain still lingered, which was not entirely unlike an ill-maintained aquarium.

After some searching, Mr. Clark found a stash of letters in a small, locked drawer which turned out to be love letters and explicit marriage proposals from all parts of the world. There must have been signatures from thirty or more women, all proclaiming their love for captain Strobeck, and all unanimously begging him for one more night in his famous "compartment".

You are like a drug Bill. Always and forever, in your compartment -

***

www.ingramcontent.com/pod-product-compliance
Lightning Source LLC
Chambersburg PA
CBHW021140080526
44588CB00008B/151